Our Yard on 2625 East Cedar Avenue and Other Stories and Poems

Trish Schreiber

Order this book online at www.trafford.com
or email orders@trafford.com

Most Trafford titles are also available at major online book retailers.

Print information available on the last page.

ISBN: 978-1-4907-6084-1 (sc)
ISBN: 978-1-4907-6085-8 (hc)
ISBN: 978-1-4907-6086-5 (e)

Library of Congress Control Number: 2015915025

Trafford rev. 09/11/2015

 www.trafford.com
North America & international
toll-free: 1 888 232 4444 (USA & Canada)
fax: 812 355 4082

INTRODUCTION

These are stories I've written over several years. Some were written for memoir classes. Others I wrote just to try to recapture a period in my life. I feel that if you read this book, you will know me.

BEDTIME

Some of my earliest memories are about sharing a room with my younger sister, Margaret. In the family, we were known as the little girls. My older sisters Katie and Elizabeth were the big girls, and Rich, the oldest, was in a league of his own. All the bedrooms at our house on Cedar Avenue were upstairs. Margaret's and my room was in the front of the house and had windows that looked out on the front yard. Our house had been built in the 1920s, and the rooms were large and airy. Our room had a walk-in closet with a built-in set of drawers. On top of the drawers was a small wooden platform. Margaret and I liked to climb up there and sit and look out the little closet window.

My sister and I had twin beds. My bed was along the front wall near a window. I could lie in bed and look out at the branches of the big old elm trees that surrounded our house. In the summer, the window would be open, and if you woke up early enough right before dawn, you could hear all the birds, as if on cue, start singing at once. I've never experienced this phenomenon in any other place I've lived.

Margaret's bed was across the room on the opposite wall. In the space between our beds, there was a table and a rocking chair where my parents would sit and take turns reading to us at bedtime. My mom liked reading the classics: *The Secret Garden*, *Heidi*, *Tom Sawyer*, *Huckleberry Finn*, and my favorite, *The Little Princess*. My dad especially loved reading Frank L. Baum's *Oz* books. He had a clear, deep voice and a wonderful way of reading out loud. After the reading installment was over, Margaret and I would recite the Lord's Prayer. Then my mom would kiss us each and add a butterfly kiss, a quick flick of her eyelashes on our cheeks. Then she would turn off the light and leave our door slightly ajar so we could see the reassuring glow of the hall light.

Even with all these loving rituals, there was a period in my childhood when I dreaded bedtime. I'm not sure at what age I began to worry about getting polio. I know my fears came directly from two things I saw on TV. The first was an episode of *This Is Your Life*. The program honored a little girl with polio who had spent time in an iron lung. The pictures of her in the iron lung really scared me. The other piece on television was a public service spot about polio. As I remember, it showed a boy playing in his front yard. Suddenly, he falls down, and then his mother screams and runs to pick him up. The idea that polio could strike me that fast was terrifying. I never shared my fear with anyone. Maybe I felt they would think it was dumb. After the bedtime rituals were done and the light was turned out, I can remember lying in my bed, worrying about getting polio. I just couldn't get to sleep. Then I would whisper over to Margaret's bed, "Margaret, are you awake? Do you want to tell stories?" I couldn't admit to my younger sister I was scared and wanted to be distracted so I could fall asleep. Sweet Margaret would usually accommodate me, though I'm sure she probably just wanted me to leave her alone and let her rest. Eventually, though, I'm not sure why, I lost my fear of contracting polio. I will always be grateful to Margaret for her little whispered stories, which helped me to go to sleep.

FAMILY DINNERS

The smell of fresh mint transports me back to my childhood. In the summer, my mom would brew Lipton tea; and at dinner, each place was set with a tall glass of iced tea on a saucer. There was also a plate with lemon wedges and sprigs of fresh mint, the sugar bowl and, of course, long silver iced teaspoons. Every member of the family mixed their tea a bit differently. I liked two spoonfuls of sugar, a squeeze of lemon, and mint leaves, which I rubbed between my fingers to release their special flavor.

Dinner at the Shannon house was pretty elegant. We ate in the dining room. The table was always set with a nice linen tablecloth. China and silver were used every evening. My mom did use paper napkins, but even these were the big heavy white ones. My mother sat at one end of the table with my younger sister, Margaret. Dad sat at the other end or head of the table. My brother, Rich (the oldest), sat to Dad's right, and Katie (the second oldest) to his left. I sat next to Katie, and Elizabeth, the middle child, sat across from me. We always had the same seats, and I know if you were to ask any one of us, we would remember the exact seating arrangement.

At dinner, there were a few hard and fast rules. You had to wear shoes at the table. There was "no singing" at the table. If you passed the salt, you weren't supposed to hand it directly to the person because you would lose their friendship. This was a family superstition, and we all adhered to it religiously. Also, you had to ask "May I please be excused?" before you were allowed to leave the table. I remember it was torture to hear the neighborhood kids outside playing and riding their bikes, while we had to sit at the table and wait to be excused. In the summer, we always played outside in the evening. Our favorite games were kick the can, hide-and-go-seek, and swing the statue.

Anyway, back to the table. I was born in 1950, so our family dinners took place in the '50s and '60s. When I was a young child, we had a live-in maid, Fannie, who cleared the table and did the dishes. At some point, Fannie got married, and though she still worked for the family, she was no longer there at dinner. So my sisters and I took over the job of doing the dishes. My mom always did all the grocery shopping and cooking. She made great meals. The dinners consisted of some kind of meat, vegetables, salad, rolls, and potatoes or rice. Almost every night, we had a dessert. There were two wonderful bakeries in Denver: Bauers and Volmers, and Mom bought many goodies from both of them. She also did a lot of baking: pies, cakes, and one time even Baked Alaska. We were always encouraged to join the Clean Plate Club. Cleaning my plate was never a problem for me. I loved all that great food.

My mom set the table and the stage for the family to be together. Dinner was a time when family things were discussed. I can remember dinners when we were all laughing so hard we couldn't stop. I remember birthday dinners where you got to pick your favorite foods followed by the traditional chocolate cake with chocolate icing, my grandmother Shannon's recipe. I can also see my little mom enjoying a cigarette after dinner. It was a habit she could never break but would hide it in her later years.

Serious things also happened at dinner. I remember Dad telling Margaret and me that my sister Elizabeth was pregnant and that she was going to drop out of Stanford and marry her high school boyfriend. There was such sadness and defeat in Dad's voice when he made the announcement. Later, when I would come home from college, there were arguments between my dad and me about Vietnam, U.S. imperialism, racism, sexism, and all the other isms I was discovering out in California. Those memories aren't as happy, but they are all part of the family history.

I could never live up to the standard my mom set, but I have established our own Schreiber dinner traditions. We eat in the kitchen on the kitchen table. The plates are plastic. We all created our individual plates with our own drawings on them using a kit called Create a Plate. We use flatware, paper napkins, and plastic glasses. Eating in the dining room with a tablecloth, china, and sliver are reserved for holiday dinners and company. We too have our seating spots. Our only hard-and-fast rule is no TV during dinner. The kids don't have to ask to be excused. But they usually say, "Thanks for the great dinner, Mom." I love that.

Like my mom, I make big good dinners. We don't have dessert, but I always have fresh fruit, which is eaten at the end of the meal. Everyone shares what has happened during the day, and we have some great discussions. Now that our oldest son, Jimmy, is off at college, the family is starting to shrink, but four is still a good group. I don't like to think about three and then just two.

Of course, on some nights, dinner together is impossible. But my husband, Jim, and the kids know how important having dinner together is to me, so they try hard to make it home. Jimmy was born in 1979, Meg in 1981, and Rich in 1985. So the Schreiber family dinners have taken place in the '80s and the '90s. My great hope is that my kids will remember their childhood meals with the same fondness that I remember mine.

I still drink iced tea, but now it is the instant kind, presweetened with NutraSweet. We have some mint growing down by the creek on our property. I think I'll put some sprigs on the table tonight. It will be a nice touch.

MY BEARS

Beary was the first, a very little white stuffed Steiff teddy bear. I bought him at Anderson's Toyland, the beautiful big blond brick toy store in Cherry Creek Shopping Center. His arms and legs could be moved forward and backward, and his head swiveled from side to side. The most endearing thing about him were his shiny black eyes, two small metal buttons. Black embroidery thread marked his nose and mouth.

I think I was about seven years old when I got Beary. Dolls had never interested me, but I always loved stuffed animals. Just looking at Beary, I felt I knew his personality. I imagined he was a sweet, shy little young bear. It wasn't long before I went back to Anderson's and bought another small bear, this time a black-and-white panda whom I named Jerry. He struck me as a more outgoing, rambunctious little fellow.

In the coming months, I got Larry, Harry, Gary, and Tet Tet Teddy to make a total of six bears. I fashioned for them an elaborate bear house out of a cardboard box and filled it with miniature furniture, which I also made out of cardboard. I invented a life story for the bears. They were a family. Larry, Harry, and Tet Tet Teddy were a slightly larger style of Steiff bear, and they were the adults of the family. Larry was the father figure and head of the family. Harry was more domestic and motherly. Harry and Larry were best friends. Beary and Jerry were best friends. That left Tet Tet Teddy and Gary as sort of a couple, although Tet Tet Teddy was an adult, and Gary was young, like Beary and Jerry.

Besides playing with them in their bear house, which I had set up in my bedroom, I took them outside. I made cool little forts for them out of sticks and leaves. The outdoor life was somewhat hard on the little animals. I don't remember how it happened, but Jerry lost both his ears. I replaced them with two small black rocks from our newly re-asphalted driveway.

I played with the little stuffed bears for years, taking them on every family vacation in a special plastic case. Once, I lost Beary on a train trip my family was taking from Denver to Sun Valley, Idaho. My sisters helped me frantically search the Pullman sleeper compartment until we found the little white bear. He was wedged between the wall and the mattress of the upper pull-down bunk. I was so relieved to find Beary. I guess because to me he was real.

It wasn't until I went to high school that I finally dismantled the bear house and relegated the bears to a spot on my bookcase. Eventually, they got packed away in a box. I didn't take them to college, but when my parents moved out of our childhood home on Cedar Avenue, I again took possession of them.

Looking at the small threadbare bears today brings back so many happy memories. I can still identify with that little girl who loved her bears.

SCARY MOVIE

When I was young, going to a movie was a big deal. There were five big movie theaters in Denver at that time, and they were all in the downtown. The Center, the Denver, the Paramount, the Aladdin, and I can't remember the other one. Sometimes I would go to the movies with my mom and sisters to see a film, but the times I enjoyed the most were when I went to the movies with my neighborhood friends Sara Gerber and Ellen Lowen. One of our mothers would drive us down and drop us off in front of the theater and then pick us up after the movie. It was so exciting to go into the big old theaters with their plush carpets and chandeliers. I loved the smell of popcorn and the whole movie experience. We usually saw Disney films or Jerry Lewis movies. My favorite movie was *The Parent Trap* with Haley Mills. I went to see it with Ellen Lowen, and we got in trouble because we didn't leave after the film was over. We stayed to watch the beginning again, and by the time we finally came out, my mom was frazzled and worried after driving around and around the block.

I don't know why we decided to go and watch *The Pit and the Pendulum*, and I don't know why our parents OK'd the movie. Anyway, Sara, Ellen, and I went down to the Denver Theater on a typical summer day. We decided to sit up in the balcony, which was unusual for us. Things started out fine with the showing of the previews and a cartoon, but when the film came on, I was almost immediately frightened. I had never been to a horror film before. I really wasn't prepared to be so scared.

I don't remember a lot about the movie, except that it was set in a castle with a torture chamber down in the dungeon. The music in the film was weird and eerie. Several scenes were done in a bloody red color. Vincent

Price starred in the film, and there were several close-ups of his devilish face. The suspense built throughout the film. I have heard people say that it is "fun to be scared." Well, I know for me it wasn't fun. At one point, a torture chamber of nails was swung open to expose an awful long-haired skeleton. I really jumped out of my seat when that happened. I think from that point on, I closed my eyes for rest of the movie; unfortunately I could still hear the creepy music.

Finally, the film was over. We left the theater and walked out into the beautiful sunshine. Once we were outside, I felt a lot better. Sara and Ellen didn't seem to be as affected by the movie as I had been. They chattered about different scenes in the movie as Mrs. Lowen drove us home. Even hearing them talk about the film made me scared. I wished I had never seen the stupid *Pit and the Pendulum*. That night, I couldn't stop thinking about the film. I shared a room with my younger sister, Margaret, and I kept talking to her after the lights were out, trying to stave off my fears. I imagined that the horrible-looking skeleton was under my twin bed. I was truly and purely afraid. Margaret was sympathetic, but eventually, she fell asleep, and I was alone with my fears. I finally, gathered up all of my courage and jumped out of bed and ran across the hall to my parents' room. Both Mom and Dad woke up, and we talked about the movie. They tried to reassure me that the movie wasn't real and that I was safe. Mom walked me back to my room, and she slept at the foot of my bed until I went to sleep.

My fears were slow to fade. I can honestly say I was scared for at least a year after seeing the film. Somehow my feeling of security was shattered by a second-rate Hollywood production. I've since read Edgar Allen Poe's "The Pit and the Pendulum." I can't seem to find much similarity between his story and the horrible movie that scared me so much back in the '50s. I've often thought about finding a copy of the movie and watching it now that I'm a grown adult. To tell you the truth, though, I don't think I want to take the chance of being scared like that again.

My Best Christmas Memory

Every year, for as long as I could remember, I always asked for a puppy for Christmas. We had a family dog, Barney. He was a sweet old dog, but he mainly just slept in the sunny spot on the living room carpet. I fantasized about having a furry puppy that would play with me. Of course, I reassured my parents, I would take care of the little dog. I promised I would feed, brush, and train him. I recruited my younger sister to also beg for a puppy. Margaret always asked for a horse, but I convinced her that our parents would never buy her a horse, but there was a chance we might get a puppy.

At our big old house on Cedar Avenue, Christmas officially started when my dad carried the cardboard boxes containing all our beloved decorations up from the basement. The five of us children all helped to "deck the halls." Every decoration had its traditional spot in the house and evoked a flood of happy memories. The manger scene was placed on a low table in the living room, and all of us kids enjoyed arranging the figures in different ways.

We never bought our tree until a week before Christmas. All of us piled into our Mercury station wagon and headed for Colorado Boulevard, which was the best place to find a tree in Denver. Many times, we would go to several lots before we all agreed on the "perfect tree." Once the tree was in the house, the wonderful smell of pine filled the air. Dad always put the lights on the tree. They were the kind with the bulbs that got very hot to the touch. Those lights shone with the most wonderful, warm colors. Mom had the honor of putting on the first decoration, a fragile glass ornament, purchased when my parents were newly married. After that, we all joined in the trimming. The last thing to go on the tree was the tinsel.

In those days, the tinsel was of the heavy metal variety. I personally loved lots of tinsel, but others in the family felt it should be used sparingly.

Our Shannon family tradition was to have our turkey dinner on Christmas Eve. The only guest at this dinner was Grandmother Cather. She lived in a big apartment building near downtown. During the weeks leading up to the feast, we baked and decorated cookies. My favorite part was icing the sugar cookies. I loved adding the bright drops of food coloring to the pure white icing and stirring it in. My mom left Wonder Bread on the counter to dry out, and using this stale bread, she made the most delicious stuffing. After dinner, we would sing Christmas carols and Grandmother Cather always recited "The Night Before Christmas" from memory.

Then it was time to write our letters to Santa Claus. Now that I was ten years old, I felt I could really write a good letter explaining why I wanted a puppy. That year, in 1960, I poured out my heart to Santa (my parents). Then we hung up our stockings and put cookies out for Santa. After all these traditional activities were completed, it was time to drive Grandmother back to her apartment. To our delight, it was one of those magical years when it snowed on Christmas Eve. As we drove through the quiet streets, I peered out the car window, watching the tiny, glittering flakes falling in front of the streetlights.

Back at home, Margaret and I went straight upstairs to our shared bedroom. We said our prayers and Mom tucked us in and gave us each a kiss. In the darkness, I asked Margaret, "Do you think we will get a puppy?"

Margaret, always the practical one, replied, "We'll just have to wait and see. Now go to sleep."

But I was too excited to sleep. I don't know how long I had been lying there awake when I thought I heard the front door close and some muffled voices downstairs. Then, I heard the sweetest sound, a small, sharp bark. I knew then, my dream was going to come true. Of course, I wanted to rush downstairs right that minute to see our new puppy, but I knew I had to wait. That night I went to sleep, the happiest little girl in the world. That is my favorite Christmas memory.

LEARNING TO DRIVE

I wasn't one of those kids who was just dying to get my driver's license. In fact, I was scared to start driving. When I was fifteen, I was in a car accident. My sister, Elizabeth, was driving. She had stopped at a stop sign and then started into the intersection right into an oncoming car. I looked up to see the car right in front of my face. We hit it, and I really didn't feel anything, but blood was gushing out of my broken nose.

This experience was stuck in my head, and it took a while to get over my fear. I was the type of girl who worried a lot, and eventually, I started to worry what would happen if I didn't get my license. Would my mom have to drive me around indefinitely? So finally, when I was seventeen, I decided to learn to drive. At that time, you weren't required to take driver's ed. All you had to do was get your learner's permit, and then six weeks later, you could take the driving test. My mom took me down to the big old DMV office in downtown Denver. I took the written test, which I had diligently studied for and passed it, no problem. Now I could drive accompanied by another licensed driver.

I was the fourth of five children, so my parents had already been through three other kids learning to drive. They had always hired the Acme Driving School to teach their kids the basics. The driving instructor came right to our house. I remember standing nervously on the front porch waiting for him to arrive. By far, the most memorable thing that happened during one of those driving sessions was when the instructor told me to take a left. I guess there was a choice between a hard left and another street that was on a left angle. I took the hard left and was heading down a one-way street going the wrong way. It took a few seconds for the instructor to realize what was going on, and when he did, he slammed on the brakes on his side of the car. He yelled at me to pull over and then had me switch places with him. I started crying and was all shook up. He said it was his fault, and I shouldn't worry. But, of course, I did.

I had four more lessons with Acme, and then I started driving with my mom in her big green Buick. She tried her best to act relaxed, but she was constantly sucking in her breath and pushing her right foot down on the floorboard. This didn't do much for my confidence. My sister, Katie, who was five years older than me, also let me drive with her. One evening, she suggested that I drive with her over in the Cherry Hills neighborhood, an area of beautiful old homes. I felt I was doing some of my best driving, until several cars started honking and flashing their lights at me. Neither Katie nor I had realized I was driving in the growing darkness without turning on the headlights.

Finally, Mom said she thought I was ready to take the driving test to get my license. The plan was to go to the Littleton DMV because it was in a rural area without much traffic. We drove out there, only to discover that since I had taken my learner's permit test at the Downtown DMV, I was required to take my driver's test at the same office, which was right in the middle of the busy downtown area. I was devastated. I started crying and falling apart. I said we should just forget it. My dear little mom, with her unlimited patience, talked and talked to me, reassuring me I would do OK at the Downtown DMV. She said we should just drive directly there. She didn't want me to put it off any longer.

I can really remember how scared and nervous I was. The area around the Downtown DMV was very congested and had several traffic lights and one-way streets. The test got off to a bad start. While the car was parked, the officer asked me to put on the brakes, so he could check to see if the brake lights worked. Instead, I put my foot on the gas. The engine roared and exhaust blew in the examiner's face. Fortunately, the rest of the test went better, and although I did make a few more mistakes, at the end of the test, miracle of miracles . . . I passed!

TRIP TO COLORADO SPRINGS

Every Wednesday morning, Dad drove me to school because Mom had her bowling league that day. On the way to Merrill Junior High, we picked up my friend, Joyce at her modest apartment building. The route to school took us by the on-ramp to Interstate 25 South. It became a running joke with us that Dad would say, "Do you want to skip school today and go to Colorado Springs?"

Joyce and I went along with the joke. We always answered that we "would love to go to Colorado Springs." We never thought too much about it. So it came as a total surprise when one Wednesday, after Dad asked his usual question, and we gave our standard affirmative reply, Dad turned on to the highway.

We spent the day in Colorado Springs. First, we had lunch at the elegant garden themed restaurant in the Broadmoor Hotel. I had my favorite, a club sandwich and a Coke. Then we visited the Cheyenne Mountain Zoo. The zoo was pretty deserted, being a Wednesday and all. We had great fun walking around the hilly zoo, observing the beautiful animals. After that, it was time to drive back to Denver.

After dropping Joyce off, we drove home. It was about five o'clock, Dad parked the Cadillac in the garage, and we went up the old cement stairs through the back porch and into the kitchen. My little mom was sitting at the kitchen table smoking a cigarette. Butts and ashes filled the glass ashtray in front of her. "Where have you been?" she asked. "The school called to see why Trisha was absent, I didn't know what to say. Of course, I called the office and found out that you hadn't come to work. I wasn't really worried, but I was wondering what was going on. Where were you all day?"

Sheepishly, my dad explained about our spur-of-the-moment trip to Colorado Springs. He apologized for any worry he might have caused my mother.

Our impromptu trip to Colorado Springs eventually became a family legend, not because it was typical of my father, but because it was such a departure from his usual personality. That day holds a special place in my memory. It was fun to do something totally unexpected, and it was great to spend time with my dad.

My Dad's Magic

I really want to preserve the memories I have of my father. I want to pass down to my children not just the facts about Dad's life, but more importantly, what kind of person he was. I guess this is what is described in all the books on writing as "to show not tell." For me though, this is so difficult. I just want to write, "My dad was a great father."

OK, I'll try to *show* you of how cool he was. Dad occasionally put on magic shows for us five kids. His tricks usually involved small gadgets. His best trick of feeding blank pieces of paper through a hand-cranked roller amazed us when first, a one-dollar bill would come out the other side, then a five-dollar bill, then a ten, and finally, a one-hundred-dollar bill! I always wondered why Dad didn't just make a bunch of money on this little machine. I totally fell for the "magic."

Speaking of magic, our family had a tradition that I think was unique to the Shannons. Every once in a while when we came to bed, our pillows would be mussed up. That's when we knew, "Magic" had come! Lying underneath our pillows we would find delicious candies and small trinkets. We never knew when to expect "Magic's" visits. Of course, when we got a little older, we realized our Dad was Magic. He would purchase his delicious surprises at an old-fashioned candy shop in downtown Denver.

Both Dad and Mom loved horse racing. In the summer, they would often spend long afternoons at Centennial Racetrack. Sometimes they would bring us kids to the track, but most of the time they just went together. We learned to always ask Dad when he and Mom came home, "How did you do at the races?".

If he had had a winning day, he would answer with a big smile, "I'm GLAD you asked." Then Dad would share his winnings, passing out one- and five-dollar bills. He always wanted to spread around his good luck. These are just few examples of why it was so much fun growing up with my magical dad.

MY DAD

Both my parents influenced me greatly: my mom in a quiet way, and my dad with his authoritative but generous manner. Dad went by a few different names. In business, he was the serious, Richard Stoll Shannon Jr. To my mom and his friends, he was Dick. His sisters, my aunts, always lovingly called him Bud. And of course, to his five children, he was known simply as Dad.

Dad was a little over six feet tall and very handsome. His hair turned gray at an early age, and I only saw him with dark hair in old photos. He always wore glasses, and through the years, he had several different styles. My dad was a very immaculate person. He often shaved twice a day, and his cheeks were very smooth and shiny. I can remember kissing his soft cheek and smelling his tart, lime aftershave.

From an early age, all five of us kids would go to Dad's office for business meetings. I usually didn't understand the discussions very well. When we were really small, we were only required to listen. But as we got older, Dad would ask us questions. Nervously, I'd sit on the leather office chair, hoping I wouldn't be called on. Dad was trying to familiarize us with the oil business, the real estate business, and the stock market. I did get the concept that you shouldn't have "all your eggs in one basket." That was why it was important for us to have diverse investments. Also at these meetings our trust funds were discussed. This was the money we would get when we turned twenty-one.

My grandfather, R. S. Shannon, made a major oil discovery in Wyoming in 1942. The well he was drilling came roaring into production on Thanksgiving Day. From this oil field, named Elk Basin, all the Shannon fortunes flowed. My dad was the youngest and only son in his family of four children. When my grandfather died, he took on the role of managing the business for his sisters and then also for the next two generations.

Family was the most important thing to my father. In the late '60s, I was involved in the antiwar movement. All of my college friends were radicals who believed that the rich should be sharing all their wealth. When I espoused these beliefs to my dad, he told me, "Trish, you can really only worry and take care of your own family."

At the time, I thought that statement was so wrong, but as I've matured and started my own family, I see the wisdom in what he said. That's not to say that my father wasn't a generous man. He gave very generously to many charities. He was also very civic-minded. He served on the Denver water board and was appointed the manager of public works by the mayor of Denver. He was proud of these jobs, but managing the family businesses and taking care of his family were the most important things to him.

I always felt I had a wonderful childhood. Mom and Dad created a beautiful home. We went on wonderful family vacations. And though we weren't a religious family, all holidays were celebrated with gusto. On Easter, we had elaborate Easter baskets and gifts, and Christmas was a fantastic production of food and toys.

I know my father wanted me to take an interest in business and investing, but I was not a good student in anything along those lines. Luckily, my dad was very supportive of my love of art, and he always praised any artwork that I produced. He was a prolific reader, and when we were younger, he read to us every night at bedtime. Some of his favorites were the *Oz* books, *Doctor Dolittle*, *Treasure Island*, and *The Jungle Book*. He introduced me to the love of reading.

Dad parented with a combination of kindness and sternness. I know my whole life I wanted Dad's approval, but in my early twenties, you wouldn't have known that. There were some very rocky years where it looked like I was going to spend my entire trust fund—first to fund the revolution and then to keep my first husband happy. Through that period, Dad never cut off communication with me, which was probably a lifesaver.

I'm glad that I finally started to shape up before my father died. When I married Jim and we started our family, Dad was really great. He and Mom came out to California several times to visit. Dad was so interested and good with my young kids. He was disappointed that we had decided to live in California. I know he would have loved to have us settle in Denver. In a way, though, I think it helped my relationship with both my parents to have some distance between us. But when my dad developed prostate cancer right after my youngest son, Rich, was born, I felt so badly that I couldn't spend more time with my father. Dad made the decision not to undergo any treatments for his disease. Needless to say, this was a very hard thing for all of us to accept. My father had seen his father go through a long period of hospitalization before he died, and he didn't want that. Dad was steadfast in his decision. I couldn't imagine a world without my father. He had always taken care of me and everyone else in our family.

I wrote my dad a letter before he died. In it, I tried to express all the love and gratitude I felt toward him. I am so grateful that I had this chance to convey my feelings to him. The day after Dad died, before I left for Colorado to attend his funeral, I received a short handwritten note from him. He wrote that he appreciated my letter and that he loved me and was proud of me. That short letter meant the world to me and is my prized possession. It is securely stored in a safety deposit box at the Auburn Wells Fargo.

The most important things I feel Dad taught me were to have a good sense of humor, to be outgoing and friendly in social situations, to have a good marriage, and to be a caring parent. He taught me the love of gardening, reading, and music. He provided me a life of financial security, which is an incredible advantage that few people are given. I feel I had the best father that anyone could ever ask for. I miss him so much, and I wish we had more time together.

MY MOM

Margaret Cather Shannon was born in Lander, Wyoming, on August 16, 1915. Her parents were Meta Elizabeth Schaper Cather and Roscoe C. Cather. She had a sister, Virginia, who was three years older. Mom has a twin. This was one of the most important aspects of her life. Her identical twin sister was named Elizabeth. Mom's love for her twin sister was an integral part of her life. From the photos I've seen of the little twins, they were the most beautiful, sunny little babies.

I wish I had made more of an effort to learn about my mom while she was still alive. She would talk a little bit about her childhood, and it always sounded so quaint and old-fashioned to me. Mom would also talk about her days at college. She and Elizabeth attended the University of Colorado in Boulder. They both joined the Delta Gamma sorority. Mom was involved in Delta Gamma activities her whole life, and many of her best friends were her sorority sisters. I know my mom was very smart, and she was always proud that she was a Phi Beta Kappa.

I don't know too much about my parents' love story. I do know that Mom was engaged to another man when she met my father in California. She broke off that engagement when she met Dad. They were married on September 17, 1938. I think my parents truly loved each other. Their marriage was one of consideration, appreciation, and passion. I remember times when Dad got home from work and he would take Mom in his arms and kiss her right there in the kitchen by the broom closet.

Mom was a small woman. She was just five feet tall and very slim and trim. I loved the way she looked and dressed. She always wore nice clothes, even if she was just spending time at home. When my parents went out, my mom would look especially beautiful. I loved when she wore her mink coat and sparkling earrings. Joy Perfume was the scent Mom used on special occasions. Oh, what an elegant and sweet smell! It was nice to have such a pretty mom. She had her hair done once a week at the beauty parlor, and for several years, Dion did her hair. Mom always filed and painted her own nails. I can remember her sitting at the kitchen table with the nail polish remover and cotton pads, preparing her nails for another color of polish.

Besides being a pretty mom, more importantly, she was a kind, loving mother. She used patience and reason to deal with her children. All my friends would say, "Your mom is so nice." And she was.

Many of my memories of Mom involved driving in the car with her. She was a willing chauffer and drove us kids to and from Stephen Knight elementary School and Merrill Junior High. Dad always drove a Cadillac, but Mom had several different makes and models of cars through the years.

Probably the favorite of all these cars was a beautiful Mercury station wagon we called Anastasia or Stashie for short. The car was turquoise green with wood side panels. Its top was white. Mom was a good driver, but on the rare occasion she had to slam on the brakes, her arm would shoot out to protect whichever child was sitting next to her in the front seat.

Often, Mom would say, "Let's go on a picnic." She would pack our round plaid cooler with sandwiches and other goodies, and we would set off to the mountains. As I remember it, we'd look for a good spot to pull off the road. With our trusty cooler, we'd hike a little way back from the road to a big rock or stream. These simple outings in the Colorado Rockies were a lot of fun. I loved smelling the pine trees and seeing all the colorful wild flowers.

We called them leg aches. I don't know if they were growing pains or what, but the pain was real, and it would wake me up in the middle of the night. My parents' bedroom was right across the hall. I'd get out of bed and stand in the doorway of their room and say, "Mommy, I can't sleep. My leg hurts." My little mom would wake up and come back with me into the room I shared with my little sister, Margaret. She'd curl up at the foot of my twin bed in her thin negligee and stay there until I was able to fall back to sleep. This memory of my mom is one of the sweetest for me.

Mom was always somewhat in my dad's shadow. He was the head of the household, and his big personality dominated our family life. I don't think I truly appreciated my mom until I became a mother myself. Then I began to marvel at the fact she had *five* children. How had she taken care of us all and made it look so easy? Of course now I realize her life couldn't have been that easy, but she never really shared her struggles with any of us. She was a private person, and I only saw her guard come down a couple of times. One summer, I was home from college for a few days. This was during my period of being a radical, and both my parents were worried about the choices I was making. I was asleep in my bedroom at the end of hall. By this time, Margaret and I had moved to the rooms that were vacated when Katie and Elizabeth went to college. I heard a noise out on the upstairs landing. When I got out of bed to investigate, I found my mom standing at the top of the stairs in her nightgown, crying piteously. I wasn't sure what to do. "Mom, are you all right?" I asked and put my arms around her. "I'll stay home if you want me to. I'm sorry if I've made you unhappy."

Mom didn't really say anything or respond. I think the whole situation embarrassed her. As I remember it, I just went back to bed. Neither of us ever mentioned the incident. Sometimes I almost felt that it was a dream. But I knew that it did happen, and I also knew that my mom had some deep sorrows that she never shared.

I can't really sum up what my mom meant to me. She did everything to make a wonderful home for her children. She and my dad were a team, and though he was the leader, my mom was the one who made the household run so smoothly. I wish I could go back and tell Mom how much I admired and loved her. She was small, but her impact on my life was huge.

MY BROTHER, RICH

In our Shannon family, there were five children. My sister Margaret and I were the youngest and considered the little girls. Katie and Elizabeth were the big girls. Rich was the oldest child and the only male. He was in a class of his own. He was seven years older than me, and we didn't really hang out with each other that much. That is why this one memory is so special to me.

The year was 1964, the height of Beatlemania. Like most fourteen-year-old girls of that time, I loved the Beatles. I can remember being in the big old kitchen of our house on Cedar Avenue. I was rinsing the dinner dishes before my younger sister, Margaret, put them in the dishwasher out in the pantry. It was summertime, and Rich was home from California, where he was going to Stanford University. I can't recall exactly how it happened. Maybe Rich mentioned that he wanted to see the movie *A Hard Day's Night*, and I chimed in that "I REALLY" wanted to see it too. Anyway, somehow it was decided that he would take me to the drive-in to see the movie. I would be his date for the evening. He even gave me a corsage made out of a lettuce leaf.

As it turned out, it was a double date with my sister Katie and her boyfriend, Larry Ladue. Rich drove, but I'm not sure what car we were in. We were driving to the Valley Drive-In on East Evans Avenue. Larry said, "Hey, this isn't the way to the drive-in."

As he pulled into the parking lot of a liquor store, Rich replied, "This is the way I go." He returned to the car with a six-pack of Coors beer, and then we drove to the movie. I don't think Larry was too upset with this development, but Katie and I wouldn't think of drinking the beer.

This was my first time at a drive-in, and sitting up in the front seat with Rich, I felt very grown-up. Then *A Hard Day's Night* came on the big outdoor screen. I was surprised that the film was in black and white, but I quickly realized this was the perfect format to showcase my beloved Beatles. The movie was shot like a documentary, and it was different from anything I'd ever seen before. The music was so great. "Can't Buy Me Love" was my favorite song. All the Beatles looked really handsome, especially Paul.

Everyone in the car loved the movie. When it was over, I remember Rich saying that maybe he would grow his hair a little longer, "just over the collar of my shirt." The Beatles had brought us all together. I will always be grateful to Rich for that evening when he made his younger sister, a shy, adolescent girl, feel very happy.

When Ann asked me to write about a memory of Rich, this is the first one that came into my mind; but of course, there are many others. Rich was a very good brother. For me he always had an aura about him. He was handsome and wore Levis and Ivy League shirts. I think he usually wore slip-on loafers and white socks. For a time, he slicked back his hair in a style called a ducktail. At South High School, I'm sure he was one of the cool kids. Rich drove a big white Pontiac convertible with sliver pipes on the sides, the first of his sporty cars.

I remember many happy vacations with Rich, like the first time our family went to Disneyland. It was so exciting to get to go the magical place we had seen on the Mickey Mouse Club. (The TV show had several installments about the park as it was being built.) We landed at LAX and then took a helicopter to Disneyland. Wow, what a way to travel. That trip was the first time Rich had a banana split at the Carnation Ice Cream Shop on Main Street.

Our other family trips were to La Jolla and Sun Valley, Idaho. In Sun Valley, in the mornings, Rich would play golf with our parents, while Margaret and I went horseback riding with a guide. Katie and Elizabeth stayed at the lodge to ice-skate on the big outdoor ice rink. We would all gather for lunch and then swim in the afternoon. I know it was fun for Mom and Dad to have a handsome son to play golf with on those trips.

My best memory of Rich as an adult was his pride in his three beautiful daughters. He seemed to love each of them in a special way for their individual talents. It is so sad to me that he wasn't in their lives longer. His wonderful daughters are his legacy to the world.

Our Yard on 2625 East Cedar Avenue

My dad went to work every weekday, dressed impeccably in a business suit and tie. But on Saturdays and Sundays, he put on his khaki shirt and pants and worked in his gardens. We had a very large yard on Cedar Avenue. There were so many different flower beds around the house, and Dad filled them all. One of the most beautiful gardens was in the front yard. A long bed was planted with perennials: peonies, lilies, goldenrod, and, in the spring, grape hyacinth and crocus. Also in the front yard, a little bit off to one side, was a round rose garden containing probably about fifteen healthy rose bushes. Dad loved roses. I know one of his favorites was the peace rose, which had big creamy white blossoms with a peach-colored blush. Throughout the summer, our house was filled with bud vases, holding one or two perfect roses. The smell of roses will always remind me of my happy childhood.

From the front porch, you could walk down a set of brick steps to the awning-covered patio on the side of the house. I know Dad planted begonias and nasturtiums in this area. Dad showed me how to taste a couple of drops of sweet nectar by tearing off the tips of the nasturtium flowers and sucking them. The patio looked out over the area we called the formal garden. In the center was a round cement lily pond encircled by a brick walk from which four red brick walkways pointed out, dividing the garden into quarters. Four weeping mulberry trees grew symmetrically around the pond. These small trees bore delicious little mulberries, and their weeping branches created great huts for us to play in. At the foot of the formal garden, there were four tall spruce trees in front of a white-latticed summerhouse. A patch of mint grew in this area.

In the summer, we would often have iced tea with dinner, and my mom would ask us kids to pick sprigs of mint to serve with the tea.

At the back of the house, the lawn went down wide hill and then leveled off. In the winter, this hill was great for sledding. In the summer, sometimes we rolled down the hill with our arms to our sides, a dizzying experience. At the bottom of the hill off to the right, there was a really large metal swing set with two swings and a chin-up bar. Margaret and I liked to play a game we called "metal plate island." The object of the game was to climb around the big metal structure without touching the ground, which we pretended was burning acid. Of course, we also liked just swinging on the swings; and since the old-fashioned set was so tall, you could really swing high. Like all kids, we bailed out of the swings when they were at their highest point. This was scary and exhilarating. Across from the swings, underneath a grove of cottonwood trees, was a drinking fountain with a white porcelain bowl. We slurped many quick drinks from that conveniently placed fountain.

At some point, Dad had extended the yard at the bottom of the hill. He added more lawn and another flower bed. In the new garden, he planted gladiolas, dahlias, and more roses. This new lawn ran the length of the full-sized tennis court, a somewhat unexpected feature of the backyard. The court was completely surrounded by a high chain-link fence. An old, ragged net ran across the middle of the court. The condition of the surface of the court was terrible. In many places, weeds pushed up through the asphalt. I can't remember anyone ever playing tennis there, but we did ride our bikes around on the old court. Along one side of the tennis court, Dad had put in strawberry plants. I can remember parting the leaves of these plants to find the delicious red berries.

On the other side of the house, there were two more summerhouses—a square one with a tile roof and a wooden one covered with grapevines. We called these two structures, the small summerhouse and the long summerhouse. My dad had a vegetable garden in this area. He grew corn, tomatoes, rhubarb, cucumbers, and raspberries. If you walked out of the small summerhouse toward the street, the vegetable garden was on the right. To the left was a beautiful rock garden on a small hillock. Dispersed among the low-growing shrubs and plants were a few pieces of petrified wood. The largest one was a three-foot tall stump. The brick red bark was perfectly preserved in stone, and the center looked like a large, colorful agate. Another shorter petrified stump had a center made up of white crystals. Margaret and I would often play in the rock garden, climbing on the ancient pieces of wood.

A walkway made up of large rectangular pieces of white marble led from the small summerhouse to the long summerhouse. The long summerhouse was an open structure made out of white-painted wood. Concord grape vines climbed up the sides and over the roof. The grapes were bitter, but we would pop the skins off and eat them. Flower beds containing iris flanked the long summerhouse on either side. I can remember my dad assigning me the job of cutting the dead iris flowers off the plants. I liked to imagine I was a poor servant girl, slaving away at the king's castle, while I was doing this task. Coming out of the long summerhouse was another marble walkway, and at the end was a wooden arch covered with a clematis vine. In the spring, a riot of purple flowers bloomed on the arch.

Our house was set back quite away from the street. A strip of grass ran parallel to Cedar Avenue and then a border of lilac bushes protected the front yard from the street. The house had a circular driveway. At both entrances, tall stucco posts stood like sentries. A plaque with our address, 2625, was displayed on the second post. The front yard was a large grassy area. Noble old elms ringed the lawn. Near the street, a tall catalpa tree grew. In the early summer, the tree was covered with white orchidlike blossoms. We would gather these flowers and make leis.

The asphalt driveway was wide enough for two cars. At the front of the house, the red cement stairs led down from the front porch to a brick landing. In between the bricks, soft green moss grew. A very old-fashioned metal mailbox was across the driveway from the house. Next to the mailbox was a snowball bush. In the spring, this shrub was covered with tight clusters of white blossoms.

This beautiful big yard was a magical place for a little girl who liked to play pretend games and play outside. Although I always appreciated the beauty of the property, I didn't really think about how much work it was to maintain the grounds until I grew up and had my own yard. Both Mom and Dad spent many hours working in the yard. Of course, they got some help with the work. A crew of Japanese gardeners came once a week to mow the lawns. In the fall, they raked up the leaves and hauled them away in giant burlap bundles. The Swingle Tree Company sprayed and maintained all the majestic trees around the house. Dad, though, did most of the gardening. He was the king of the gardens. Our yard on Cedar Avenue was his masterpiece.

MY MOST LIFE-CHANGING MOMENT

The day I left for college, my life changed forever. I was the fourth child out five in the family to go off to a university. My dad firmly believed that you should go away to school, so that's the way it was. I had decided to go to the University of California, San Diego. This choice was made mainly because my grandmother Shannon lived in La Jolla, right near UCSD, and I had applied there and been accepted.

I don't really remember the summer before I left. My main activity at that time was horseback riding. My younger sister, Margaret, and I spent almost every day at Bridle Path Stables, riding and hanging out with our friends. That summer, I taught beginning riding lessons. Also I groomed horses and saddle soaped tack for the stables' trainer, Suzy Balensienfen. Having a summer job was another one of my dad's requirements. My older brother, Rich, had worked with a landscaping crew, mowing lawns as a teenager. My two older sisters had to work at the Colorado National Bank, which they both hated. Somehow, my dad had softened up and let me work at the place I liked the best, the stables.

Anyway, the summer passed, and I can remember I didn't pack until the night before I was leaving. We went out to dinner at the Denver Athletic Club. My dad wanted the meal to be a nice farewell, but I wasn't in a very festive mood. Back at home, I packed my wool Villager skirts and matching blouses. Later, I would discover they were not the style on campus; not by a long shot. I know I waited until the last minute to pack, because I just couldn't believe I was going to leave home. I didn't want to go.

My mom and my older sister, Katie, were driving out from Denver to California with me in my two-year-old white Camaro. That was another family tradition, each of us as children got a new car when we turned sixteen. At the time, most of my stable friends were well off, and I didn't realize how unusual it was for a sixteen-year-old to have a brand new Camaro. The plan was that Katie and Mom would drive out with me, so I could have a car at school. Then they would fly home.

I can't remember packing the car or any of the last minute details. But I can remember so clearly standing in the front hallway of our big old house, saying "good bye" to my dad with tears streaming down my face. I remember the worried look Dad had. I think he realized what an innocent and inexperienced girl I was, and maybe, he was regretting his own "go-away-to-school rule." I recall walking through the front door out onto the red painted cement porch and down the brick steps. I was leaving home. I was really leaving home. Even as I squeezed into the backseat of the Camaro, I just couldn't accept it was happening. My life was going to change.

Now my daughter, Meg is a senior, and she is trying to decide and figure out where she will go to college. When she asks me, "How did you decide where to go?" How can I explain I didn't really decide. I didn't know what I wanted to do. I went away to school because I was expected to go. My parents pushed me out of the nest, and I began the scary, exciting journey to becoming an adult.

CALLING HOME

My parents and I had agreed that I would call home every Thursday evening at seven o'clock. At first, I had been so homesick that I wanted to call more often. But Dad had suggested the once-a-week schedule. I now realize he wanted me to become more independent and to adjust to my new life as a college student. I don't think either of us could imagine how many things would change for me during my first year of college at UCSD.

That Thursday, calling home in the middle of everything that was going on seemed surreal. All day long, throngs of students had clogged the Plaza, listening to an array of anti-war activists. The speakers were calling for a student strike to oppose the war in Vietnam. I left the crowd and went up some steps to a wide terrace in front of the Revelle Library. There, a low, modernistic cement structure housed four pay phones, each one in its own little cubicle, allowing the caller some quiet and privacy.

This entire spring quarter, my calls home had become more and more awkward as I tried to explain my new feelings and ideas to my parents. After putting in my dime, I dialed zero, then the area code and our home phone number in Denver. The operator came on, and I said, "I'd like to place a collect call from Trish."

My dad answered the phone and accepted the charges. I heard the dime come tinkling down into the coin return slot. The call was connected. "Hi, Dad," I started out tentatively. "How is everything going at home?"

"Oh great, Trish, I've been able to get some good work done in the garden."

When he said that, I pictured him in his crisp khaki pants and shirt, kneeling down among his roses.

My mom got on the extension, and after a few pleasantries, she said, "I think it is just awful all these demonstrations that are going on at colleges. Students are there to learn not to demonstrate. I can't imagine why anyone would pay tuition for their children, when they are acting like that."

"Well, Mom, I think kids see that our country is involved in a—" I searched my mind for the right words, "in a bad war."

"You think fighting communism is a bad cause?"

"But, Mom, the war isn't really about that, the U.S. is an imperialist country, we are just trying to control Southeast Asia for our own profits." I was repeating the beliefs that I had heard so many times, since I'd started my classes last fall. How could I convey to my parents the turmoil that I had been going through? How could I explain that most of my childhood beliefs about our country were being challenged? Like most American kids, I had always thought of the United States as the good guys. Here at the University of California San Diego, in the spring of 1969, that was not the popular opinion.

"Trish, your mother and I are just concerned about you. Maybe it was a mistake to have you go out to California for college. I know you really wanted to stay closer to home. I was the one who encouraged you to go out of state."

"No, Dad, I'm glad I came out here, but everything is so different. It's not just how I feel about the war, I'm confused about a lot of things. Like why do I have so much, when other people don't have anything?"

I heard my mom sigh with exasperation, "Trisha, I'll talk to you next week. I have to get back to my crossword puzzle."

"Oh, OK, Mom. I love you."

"Listen Trish, this is hard for your mother and for me too. We respect that your ideas are changing that's part of growing up. I think you'll find though, as you get older, that you can't change the whole world. All you can really do is take care of yourself and your family."

I wanted to argue, to point out that his ideas were selfish. I wanted to say that it was wrong not to want to fight injustice. But instead, I just said, "I love you, Dad. I'll talk to you next week."

"I love you too, goodbye, sweetheart."

I gently put the receiver back in its cradle. A warm breeze brought with it the smell of the ocean. I stood up and walked back down to the Plaza—back to my new friends, my new ideas, and my new life.

THE WAR IN VIETNAM

I've often wondered how my college experience would have been different if I hadn't gone to school in the turbulent late '60s. I was the most innocent and inexperienced girl when I set out for college in California from my home in Denver, Colorado. My dad thought it was important that all of his five children go away to school. I definitely would have been happy to stay at home, but I knew what was expected, so I half-heartedly applied to some out-of-state schools. One of my choices was the University of California at San Diego. My grandmother Shannon lived in La Jolla, which was near the campus, and I figured I could visit her.

My mom drove out with me because my parents were allowing me to have my car at college. During the orientation, it was discovered that I had never sent in my housing deposit and as a result, I didn't have a dorm room. (This probably happened because I had ignored all the mail from the college, since I was in denial that I would actually go there.) The dorms were incredibly crowded, and there was no space for me at that late date.

Anyway, understandably, my mom was upset and stood up in one the parents' meetings and complained. Another mom attending the meeting offered to have me come live at their house and share their daughter Kathy's room. Amazingly enough, this proved to be the solution, so instead of moving into a dorm, I moved in with the Kitches, a family with five kids who lived in La Mesa. I adjusted pretty well to living in the big sprawling ranch house with my new family. Kathy and I became close friends. She was incredibly generous in sharing her room with me. We had different class schedules so we usually didn't take the thirty-minute long drive to school together.

That first quarter, I had an English class, a math class and Theories of Philosophy 101. This philosophy class really blew my mind. Not only did Professor Kane talk about Socrates and Plato, but he also stood in front of the auditorium of young students and talked about U.S. imperialism and the unjust war in Vietnam. Now, I had always been taught, all through school that we were the good guys. The idea that the U.S. government was going into other countries for the benefit of big corporations was totally foreign to me. All these new ideas were different from what I had thought before. I was having a very difficult time trying to reconcile everything in my head. When I came across the idea that what you believe is relative to your frame of reference, that concept made a lot of sense to me. I figured I needed to expand my frame of reference and UCSD was certainly the place to do that.

There were three main issues of the day: the war in Vietnam, racism in America, and the women's liberation movement. The antiwar movement was the one I became most involved in, but I was strongly affected by the other two also.

Kathy, like me, was experiencing a lot of changes. She started dating a friend of one of her TAs, and she really wanted to move out of her parents' house. I would have been happy to stay living with the Kitches, but Kathy really wanted to leave, so as result, the second half of my freshman year, Kathy and I moved into a house with three other girls in Del Mar. In this house, I was a fish out of the water. The three older girls were all sleeping with their boyfriends, and when Kathy's boyfriend started staying over with her in the room right next to mine, I actually started sleeping up on the flat roof of the house to get away from it all. That first year of college was such a radical change for me that at times I just couldn't believe where I was and what I was doing. I thought, "Who am I?"

I started going to SDS (Students for a Democratic Society) meetings. By this time, I had become convinced that the war in Vietnam was wrong, and I felt it was my duty to protest the war. Besides that, at these meetings, there were a lot of people I thought were cool. These student radicals were to become my friends. They would be the people I would work with, live with, and love for the next few crazy years of my life.

COLLEGE LETTER

My sister, Elizabeth, mailed me this letter in 1999 with an enclosed note that said, *Trisha, Found a lot of letters in some boxes from Mom's house. Thought you might like to have this. Love, Elizabeth.*

Dear Mom and Dad, December 8, 1970

Isn't this a change from the old notebook paper? (*I had done a little drawing of a horse and apple trees on the top of the letter.*) I don't really have any interesting news so at least I thought I'd try to spruce up my stationery. Things at school have been OK. I just have sort of a routine, which is fairly pleasant but I just get dissatisfied with everyday stuff. I realize I'm really unrealistic—I mean I know everything isn't always going to be great. I just keep feeling useless, and yet I don't find anything that I really feel is useful. I know you must want to just yell at me and say get organized and stop complaining, but Mom and Dad I'm trying.

It's easy for you to say or admit that you've sheltered me but just because I realize I've been sheltered doesn't make me automatically ready to face everything. It's hard for me to handle all my freedom. I want someone to tell me what to do—but it has to be something I want to do. I'm not sure that there is anything I want to do—anything I want to work at. I know this is a terrible attitude and that I must do something and do it well. I guess what this leads up to is I don't know what I'm doing next quarter or even at Christmas. I'm being as truthful as I can even though I know it's not the stuff you want to hear. I wish I wasn't worrying and disappointing you but I don't want to lie to you about how I'm feeling right now . . . stuck between idealism and realism. I'll call soon but I don't want to call until I have something to say. I can't even escape through the ways everyone else does because I don't accept them as good. Oh well, I hope you guys are fine and everything.

Love,

Trish

I copied this letter word for word. I can still relate to that mixed up nineteen-year-old girl. The next few years were difficult ones, but I made it through.

So Dizzy

I opened my eyes, and a wave of nausea hit me. I felt saliva seeping into my mouth and realized I was going to throw up. After vomiting, I shakily went back to bed. I was surprised that I didn't feel any better after throwing up. In fact, I felt even worse. Every time I opened my eyes, the ceiling was spinning around. Closing my eyes helped, but how long could I stay in bed with my eyes closed?

At age twenty-two, of course, I had had several cases of twenty-four-hour stomach flu in my life, but I knew this was different. I just felt so dizzy, and if I moved around at all, I would be sick to my stomach. Don, my husband, was concerned about me. We had only been married a few months. I was going to the College of Arts and Crafts in Oakland, and Don was running his own business, Cobra Performance. I had given Don the money to purchase his business from my trust fund, which I received when I turned twenty-one. We were living in a house that we had just bought (again with my trust fund money) in Concord, California. Anyway, I told Don to go to work. I would be OK.

In the middle of the day, the phone rang. It was my sister, Katie, calling from Denver. In our family, we never liked to admit that we were sick, so when I answered the phone, I tried to sound normal. Katie could tell right away though that I was sick. "You sound terrible," she said with sympathy in her voice. I explained my symptoms, but even talking made me nauseous, so it wasn't a very long conversation.

By the next day, I was no better, and I had thrown up more times than I could count. Don found a doctor's number in the phone book and made an appointment for that afternoon. Before we left for the doctor, my mom called. She had heard from Katie that I was sick, and she was really worried. I wished she were there with me. This was really the first time I had been sick away from my parents. My mom said, "Trish, I think you might have vertigo. I had it once several years ago and it really knocked me out. My doctor prescribed something called Antivert, which is for motion sickness."

"Thanks, Mom, I'll ask the doctor about it," I replied.

Going to the doctor was an ordeal. I was sick in the car, although by this time, there wasn't much to throw up. Don had to practically carry me from the car to the doctor's office. In the examining room, I was sick again. The doctor said I had a problem with my inner ear causing dizziness. My mom's diagnosis of vertigo was correct. "What causes it?" I asked.

The doctor looked at me kindly and said, "We don't really know, but it can be related to stress." He prescribed some medicine for the nausea and also the Antivert, which really seemed to help.

In a couple of days, I was feeling better. But a tiny part of me acknowledged that I knew what the stress was that had caused me to get sick. I was married to a guy I really didn't love or trust. I was away from my family, and I was unhappy. My body knew before I did, that I was in trouble.

MY MARRIAGE

Last Saturday was our anniversary. Jim and I have been married twenty-eight years, which seems like a long time, but I would still describe our marriage as a work in progress. It's not that we are constantly thinking about breaking up. We're definitely not. It is just that sometimes I think we both feel things could be better between us.

I met Jim at a bar in Walnut Creek. My friends Pam and Bob had taken me out to try to cheer me up. I had very recently separated from my husband, Don, who I had been married to for less than a year. Another girl went out with us that night. Her name was also Trish. She was the sister of one of Don's friends. On the way to the bar, she told me that she had slept with Don on the first night that he moved out of our house in Concord. I couldn't believe it. Needless to say, I was at a low point.

The bar was called the Mine Shaft. Jim was there with his brother, Bill. They were on a vacation from Chicago, visiting their older brother, Dick, and his family. I think Bill actually approached our table first, but then I also met Jim. He didn't ask me to dance, which turned out to be true to his character, since he doesn't like to dance. He told me his name. I heard Shriver, not Schreiber. I thought to myself he might be connected to the Kennedys. He asked me for my phone number. I gave it to him, but I really doubted that he would ever call me. But he did.

The next few days were a whirlwind of romance, and by that, I mean sex. Jim had to go back to Chicago, and again, I doubted that he would come back. But he did. I moved out of the house I was buying with Don and rented a small house. When Jim came back, we started living together.

Our life together started with passion. I couldn't believe I was with such a tall and handsome guy.

We got engaged one year after we met and then got married back in Denver about six months after that. We bought a green Chevy van and took a road trip the summer after we were married. That was probably the beginning of my tradition of backseat driving. This is one of the aspects of our marriage that Jim isn't crazy about. Of all the places we saw on our travels, the Sierra foothills seemed like the best place to live, and we decided to move there.

The best part of our marriage has been having our three kids. I know we always felt so proud and lucky that our children were healthy, attractive, and intelligent. Of course, we had some differences of opinions on parenting. But I think we were always able to come together when it really counted. Both Jim and I enjoyed being involved in the kids' school and sporting events. It was a big adjustment for us when they went off to college and were out of the house.

Throughout our marriage the same few issues have caused problems. One thing is thing that has bothered me is that Jim doesn't like getting gifts. Gift-giving was always a big deal in my family, and it's taken me a long time to accept that Jim just doesn't like gifts. I've given up trying to find the perfect present. Another cause for discord is my restlessness. I feel guilty if I'm not accomplishing something, even if that something is really just busy work that really means nothing. Jim on the other hand *can* sit and relax and not feel badly about it. This really bugs me at times, especially now that he is retired and home much more. Jim's sense of humor is a plus and a minus in our relationship. He has a great wit, and most of the time, we find the same things funny. At times though, his take on things is just too sarcastic.

A few weeks ago, we went down to Arizona to visit our daughter, Meg. We drove through Oak Tree Canyon, which is between Flagstaff and Sedona. The scenery was incredibly spectacular. I looked over a Jim in the driver's seat. I realized I was so happy to have someone sharing all this beauty with me. Someone who knows me inside and out. Someone I can count on. I guess that is what marriage is in the end.

Everything Changed

I had a very easy pregnancy. My husband, Jim, and I went to Lamaze classes in preparation for the big day. We watched a film of a birth, and one man in the class fainted and fell right off of his chair. He hit the floor with a loud thud. I didn't faint, but it did seem somewhat unbelievable to me that I would actually be going to go through the process I was seeing up on the screen. When the time came, though, I made it through the birth with no problems.

James Robert Schreiber came into the world on January 15, 1979. From that day forward, my life was changed for the better and forever. All the clichés I had ever heard turned out to be true. I did love this little baby so profoundly and unconditionally. My life took on a completely new significance, because now I had a son who was depending on me.

At the time, we were good friends with a couple, Pam and Bob. We would play cards with them every Friday night and smoke Bob's never-ending supply of marijuana. After Jimmy was born though, I realized it didn't matter to me if I ever played cards, smoked pot, or saw Pam and Bob ever again. My priorities were totally different now. I had a new sympathy and empathy for humanity. Watching any news show about children in dire circumstances would bring me to tears.

I had absolutely no experience with babies. Babysitting had never been my thing, so I really didn't know what I was doing. It scared me to leave the hospital. When my pediatrician said to bring the baby into his office in two weeks, I couldn't believe that it would be that long before he checked him again. I had read some books in preparation for my new role as a mother. But in the end, I think just basic instincts took over.

Fortunately, Jimmy was a very calm and easy-going baby. He really didn't cry much, and he quickly got on a schedule.

My parents came out for a visit when Jimmy was about a month old. It was so great to have two other people who were as excited as I was about this wonderful baby boy. I truly believed that he was the best baby that had ever been born. Jim felt this way too, and we were probably obnoxiously proud parents.

Of course, everything about becoming a parent wasn't completely great. I certainly couldn't go places at the drop of a hat anymore. I always had to be sure I brought all the "baby supplies" with me. Also, going out with just Jim and I, became a special occasion instead of a spontaneous thing. I never really minded the lack of freedom. It seemed like a small price to pay for all the happiness our little son was giving us. Becoming a mother changed everything for me. I left the uncertainties of my twenties behind and entered the real world.

My Girl

"She's been crying quite a bit," the nurse commented as she rolled my baby's bassinet into the hospital room. "Did you have something spicy for dinner?"

I thought back to the dry roast beef with gravy that I had eaten earlier. "I don't think so," I answered.

"Well, your daughter is colicky," the nurse persisted.

Just twelve hours after her birth, I had the first clue to what the future would be like with my second child, Meg. "Colic" I had always thought was just an excuse inept mothers used when their babies were crying and they didn't know what to do. I sincerely scoffed at the idea that you couldn't easily figure out a way to stop any infant from crying. After all, when my first son was born three years earlier, I didn't know anything about infants. I'd never done any babysitting or taken care of a younger sibling. I had *no* experience, and yet Jimmy had hardly ever cried, and if he did, I quickly figured out it was because he was hungry or overly tired.

Motherhood—I was born for it. Finally, something I was good at. My breasts, which I'd resented when they started developing in about seventh grade, now had a function, a purpose. They were beautiful. Having a baby was beautiful. Motherhood was really the greatest, most profound thing that had ever happened to me. And my husband, Jim, felt the same way.

Jimmy was such a good baby. We could go to restaurants, and he would sit quietly. He was good traveler, in the car and on airplanes. Everything went so smoothly. I credited most of it to my good mothering skills: my organization, my ability to plan ahead and figure out everything my little son needed to be happy. And my success at mothering continued as he grew older. He was just an agreeable, happy kid.

So as I awaited the birth of our second child, I was much less worried that the first pregnancy. Well sure, I had those hidden fears about birth defects and Down Syndrome—possible problems that probably every mother considers. But most of my mind felt I would have another perfect, wonderful baby.

The delivery, early in the morning, had gone easily. In fact, the on-call doctor had the delivery table on a slant, so I was in sort of a sitting position. Pushing was easier than it had been with Jimmy. The baby came out, no problems, healthy, perfectly formed, *a girl*—everything I'd hoped for.

I'd spent the day in my hospital room with little Meg. Jim and Jimmy came for a visit. I tried to focus all my attention on Jimmy. I wanted to let him know he was still my important, little boy. I told him, "I'll be home tomorrow."

After dinner, the aforementioned dry roast beef, I nursed the baby, and then the nurse come in and suggested, "Why don't you let me take your baby down to the nursery, so you can get some sleep. I'll bring her back when she's hungry."

"Thanks," I said. I was tired. It had been a good day not a great day. So when the nursed brought Meg back and made her pronouncement that the baby was colicky, I thought, "No way."

"She's probably just hungry," I told the nurse. "Thank you for bringing her back in." I was an experienced mother. I knew what I was talking about. The nurse raised her eyebrows, then turned and left the room. I was alone in the semidark room with my new little daughter.

I bared my left breast and settled Meg in the crook of my arm. She latched on greedily and began to suck. "Great," I thought, wincing a little bit. I knew my nipples would toughen up in the coming days, but for now, the nursing hurts. But it didn't just hurt me, Meg would take a series of sucks and then her body would stiffen, and she would pull away from the breast and start crying—hard.

What was going on here? I tried burping her and patting her back. She continued to cry. Finally, I got out of the bed and with her in my arms started walking in circles around the hospital room. That seemed to help. However, when I tried to gently lay her back down in the bassinet, she immediately began to cry again. This was a pattern that I would come to know well. It wasn't like Meg cried all the time, but she cried *a lot*. Of course, I talked to her pediatrician about the problem. Dr. Dobbins, who looked sort of liked Dennis the Menace's father, made the same pronouncement that the nurse had given that first night. "You have a colicky baby. She gets gas, and it hurts her stomach, so she cries. We could try her on a soy formula and that might help," he told me.

"Formula, was he kidding?" I thought. Breastfeeding was so much better for the baby. Now way was I going to give up nursing Meg. With hindsight though, I think I made the wrong decision. Breast milk didn't agree with my little daughter. Often, while she was nursing, she would seem to be in pain. She hardly ever spit up, and I always sort of thought that was part of the problem. Anyway, I doggedly persisted breastfeeding Meg, and she continued to cry.

It was challenging having an active, small son and a very fussy baby. Jimmy was used to being the center of attention, and it was hard for him to adjust to the new reality. I tried to show him as much love and attention as possible and at the same time take care of Meg. One thing that calmed Meg down was movement. A lifesaver for me during this period was a snuggly cloth baby-carrier. I was able to get some of my household chores done by wearing Meg in the carrier. Jim was also a tremendous help. He would take care of Jimmy while I was dealing with Meg. It dawned on me how difficult it must be for single moms to handle all the duties of motherhood alone.

I also realized for the first time how you could be so frustrated by a baby's crying that you could be driven to doing something crazy. One day, I was carrying Meg in my arms, walking her around and around the upstairs of our house, trying in vain to get her to drop off to sleep for her nap. The circuit took me through our bedroom, our bathroom, the baby's room, and across the walkway that opened up to the living room down below. As I trudged by the railing for what seemed like the hundredth time, I thought of tossing Meg over the rail. And though it was just a brief thought and something I would never do, just the fact that I had formed the thought was so shocking and scary. I guess I gained some kind of understanding then about how people can snap and hurt their kids.

I don't know exactly when things started to improve. When Meg started to smile, that was a big help. She had the greatest smile. The expression "to light up with a smile" described her perfectly. Jimmy learned he could make her smile and laugh. He started to show more interest and love for her. By the time she was about seven or eight months old, her colicky days were behind her. Dr. Dobbins had assured me she would grow out of this phase, and he was right. Meg became a wonderful daughter with the most beautiful smile. I had learned so much about motherhood from her.

A Funny Thing Happened

When our three kids were pretty young, my husband, Jim, and I enjoyed watching *Late Night with David Letterman*. At that time, the show came on at 12:30, after the *Tonight Show* on NBC. We never stayed up that late, but instead, taped the show and watched it the next evening after the kids went to bed. We really liked Letterman's humor. We especially enjoyed the segments that involved his viewers like: "Stupid Pet Tricks," "Viewer Mail, and "Stupid Human Tricks."

I wanted to try to get on our favorite show. My first attempt was a letter to Viewer Mail. I wrote, "Dear Dave, My husband and I really enjoy your show. The only problem is that every night while we watch your show, my husband, Jim, eats a big bowl of ice cream. This would be OK, but he never washes his bowl. I thought a word from you, on national television, might get him to wash his bowl. Sincerely, Trish Schreiber, Meadow Vista, California."

I was really happy because my letter was one of the ones featured on Viewer Mail. After David Letterman read the letter, he said, "I'm sorry, Trish, I can't help you with your problem, because I also have a big bowl of ice cream every night, and I never wash my bowl either." After he said that the camera panned back to show a huge stack of dirty bowls sitting on the stage. Jim and I thought that was pretty funny.

After my letter got on the Letterman show, I wanted to try for bigger and better things. I saw my opportunity after attending a family gathering where my brother-in-law, Dick, showed us a trick he had learned at a New Year's Eve party. Dick dropped a lighted match into a small aperitif glass and then placed his cheek against the rim of the glass. This action extinguished the match and created a vacuum. Dick's cheek was sucked into the glass and the small glass was stuck to the side of his face. When I saw that trick, I thought maybe I could use it to get on *Late Night with David Letterman* for a Stupid Human Tricks segment.

I really didn't know how to go about getting on the show. But I figured I should send in a videotape of me performing the trick. First though, I had to perfect the trick. This was not easy. I found out I had to let the match burn for just the right amount of time; too short and the glass wouldn't stick, too long and it would burn my cheek. When I finally had the trick down, I asked Jim to film me doing the trick. Then I sent the tape to the address they gave out at the end of the show.

It was just an ordinary day a few weeks later, when I got a call from the show. I couldn't believe what I was hearing, they wanted me to come out to New York in just a couple of days to perform my trick on the show. I was going to be part of Stupid Human Tricks, *wow*. The lady on the phone explained that my travel expenses and hotel would be paid for by the show and that I would also be paid actors' scale ($545.00) for appearing on the show. I asked her if my husband could come with me and she said, "Yes, but you will have to pay his airfare." That was no problem since the actors' scale money would cover his ticket.

So later that week, Jim and I were off to New York on a red-eye flight. My friend, Pam, was watching our three kids. Without her, we could never have made the trip. When we landed a driver holding a sign saying "Schreiber" was there to greet us. I had never ridden in a limo before, and it was exciting to drive into the "Big Apple" this way.

That afternoon, there was a rehearsal supervised by one of the producers of the show. I met the other two people, Mark and Bill, who were also going to be doing Stupid Human Tricks. They were both young college guys. David Letterman was not around. At the rehearsal, it took me a couple of attempts to accomplish my trick. I was so nervous. It was very weird being on the *Late Night* set. Just like I'd always heard, it looked much smaller being there in person than it did on TV. After the rehearsal, we were taken to the Omni Hotel, where we would have a couple of hours to relax before the taping of the show. Jim went for a walk and some sightseeing. I stayed in the room and called my family and friends to let them know I was going to be on the *Late Night with David Letterman Show* that night.

The taping of the show started at 5:00 p.m. I expected to be waiting in the famous green room, but instead, we were told to wait in a room that looked like a storeroom. We sat on folding chairs and watched the first two segments of the show on a TV monitor. Then we were led backstage. Mark was the first to go on. His trick was wrapping his head in cotton candy. There was a cotton candy machine on the stage, and he circled around it until his head was covered in the pink confection. The audience laughed and clapped.

Then it was my turn. David Letterman said, "Is there a Trish Schreiber here? Trish Schreiber?" That was my cue. I walked out on stage carrying my aperitif glass and a book of matches. We shook hands. I tried to look right at David Letterman's face and realized that I was actually meeting the man I had watched so many times on television. He said, "Where are you from?" To my reply of "Meadow Vista, California," Dave commented, "That sounds beautiful. Where is that located?"

I nervously replied, "It's east of Auburn." Then realizing no one would know where Auburn was, I added, "It's in the foothills of the Sierras, east of Sacramento."

Then Dave asked what my trick was. I explained I would do a trick that you might do in a bar, claiming you could pick up a glass without touching it with your hands or your mouth.

Dave asked me if I went to many bars? I replied, "I wish." Then he asked me if I wanted a drum roll. I said, "A drum roll would be good."

I placed my aperitif glass on the pedestal, which had been brought on stage for my trick. I struck a match and dropped it into the glass. I carefully watched the match burn, and when I thought the time was right, I lowered my right cheek onto the rim of the glass as firmly as I could. I knew immediately that the trick had worked and worked well. My cheek was sucked down and the glass was securely attached. I raised my head with the glass sticking off my cheek, and I heard clapping and laughter. Then, in a moment of uncharacteristic acting, I pretended that I was having some difficulty removing the glass from my cheek. After a couple of phony tugs, I finally pulled it off with a pop.

David Letterman said, "Are you OK?" I replied I was fine, but I just wanted to say one thing, that my brother-in-law, Dick Schreiber, taught me the trick. Dave said, "That looks like something Dick would do." Then we shook hands again, and I walked off the stage. Once backstage, I had such a feeling of exhilaration. I was so happy and relieved that the trick had worked. It had been really great hearing the audience laugh.

The last guy Bill did his trick, which was taking a dollar bill out of his wallet with his tongue. His trick was also a big hit. After that, we were led back to the storeroom to watch the rest of the show on the TV monitor. Dave's guests that night were: Harvey Picar, an eccentric comic book author and Florence Joyner, the champion Olympic runner. Then the show was over. We were unceremoniously led to the elevator, and then we were on our own. Jim and I said "good bye" to our fellow Stupid Human participants.

We flew back to California the next day. Being on the show that November in 1988, is an experience I will never forget. Every once in awhile, I watch the videotape and relive the funny thing that happened to me.

MY ACCOMPLISHMENT

From college on, I always attended aerobics classes. Wherever I was living I would find out where classes were being taught. When we moved to Meadow Vista, I discovered a teacher named Nancy Smith taught classes in the Placer Hills School cafeteria in the afternoons. Those were some of the best times. Nancy taught what she called "jog jazz," which was a takeoff on "jazzersize." She had routines to the latest popular songs, and I loved her moves and the music she picked. Most of the women in the class were young mothers like me, and I made some good friends there. Nancy was our idol. She was so fit and always wore the cutest leotards, tights, and legwarmers. The only downside to the class was the cement slab floor in the cafeteria was a killer to the feet.

At some point, Nancy moved her classes to the Auburn Racquet Club, and of course, I followed her there. Once at the club, I started attending other people's classes. Nancy was always my favorite, but I liked and looked up to all the instructors. It was a sad day when Nancy announced that she was moving to San Diego. When I said "good bye," I told her just how much her classes had meant to me.

In my years at the Auburn Racquet Club, I saw many instructors come and go. I always liked classes with good music. I was a "regular" and attended classes on most weekday mornings. My three kids were all used to coming to the club and going into childcare while I was in class. Many times while I was in a class, I would think what I would do if I was teaching. I started to have just an inkling that I wanted to try to become an aerobics instructor. I'm not sure how long I just thought about the idea, but it was a long time. I had so many doubts about whether I could do it. I told myself that at forty, I was probably too old to start this career. Besides, I was far from thin, and I didn't look like an aerobics instructor.

One day though, I stayed after class and talked to Paula Cook, who was the head of the aerobics department at the time. I told her of my desire to become an instructor, and I also explained my reservations. She was so great. She encouraged me to give it a try and told me about an aerobics instructor course that was given at a place called the Firm in Sacramento. I signed up for the six-week course, and I was on my way. The course was held on six consecutive Saturdays down in Sacramento. My husband, Jim, agreed to watch the kids while I attended the classes. When I entered the mirrored aerobics studio, I was surprised to see I wasn't the oldest student taking the class. That was a relief. I learned a lot in those classes: anatomy, choreography, and the importance of teaching a safe class.

The next step was to try teaching a class. One of my favorite classes was dance aerobics. This class was taught by another Nancy, Nancy Bender. She was a mentor for me. First, she suggested I teach just a short portion of one of her classes. I planned to lead the class through just three songs for which I had made up routines. The night before I was going to make my debut, I was so anxious that I couldn't sleep. Standing in front of the class was one of the most intimidating things I had ever done. I didn't do very well that first time. I forgot some of the moves and became flustered. I learned a very important lesson. I needed to practice, practice, practice.

Nancy continued to let me teach portions of her classes, and I started to get better. During that time, I was also studying to take the IDEA Aerobics Instructor Certification exam. Certification was required to work at the Auburn Racquet Club. There was a thick manual, which I studied religiously. I made tapes of some of the most important definitions and listened to them while I was driving the kids around. The exam was given at Sac State, and it was hard. I anxiously awaited the results. When they came in the mail, I read my score. I had passed by just two points. Yikes!

With my certification in hand, I talked to Linda Moeller, who was now the head of the aerobics department. She said there weren't any class openings, unless I wanted to teach water aerobics. Water aerobics, that wasn't my dream. I'd never attended a water aerobics class. In fact, I didn't even like water. I knew I had to start somewhere, so I said, "I'd love to teach an aqua class." That turned out to be one of the best decisions I ever made. I learned to love the water, and I especially loved the women who came to my classes. I was able to play all the music I loved and my confidence grew.

As time passed, I was offered indoor classes. I had achieved my dream of becoming an aerobics instructor. The journey wasn't always easy. I taught many classes where only one person showed up. And I had to face the fact that not everyone liked my teaching style.

Today, my aerobics career is something I treasure. I feel so fortunate to have a job I love. I pride myself in teaching classes that are safe and always start on time. I really try to encourage my students and make my classes enjoyable. A couple of years ago, Jacqueline our current director, approached me with the idea of starting a class for older participants held up in the aerobics room. So I started teaching "low-impact aerobics." This has been my favorite class to teach. I get to use my favorite dance moves, albeit at a slower pace, and I can play my favorite music. Now that my kids are grown and out of the house, I really don't know what I would do with myself if it weren't for my aerobics career. I'm so glad I tried for it and that it worked out.

MY MOOLA

"You're rich, aren't you?" My fourth grade friend, Janet Bailey, asked me. "I heard you live in a big mansion."

Even at age nine, I felt the tug of war within myself; between wanting my friends to know my family was wealthy and not wanting them to know. So I just answered, "Well, our house is kind of big, but it's not a mansion."

Having money has defined my life. My father's father, Richard Stoll Shannon, struck oil on Thanksgiving Day, November 26, 1940. That Elk Basin discovery in Park County, Wyoming, was the source of the income that has flowed through the Shannon family down to me.

I can't remember at what age I was told that I would receive a trust fund when I turned twenty-one. Dad tried to prepare me. He periodically conducted business meetings at his office. Dad talked about stocks and bonds, real estate investments, and oil exploration. I listened, but those meetings never really prepared me for the unique position I was going to be in for my entire adult life.

I've never had to worry about having an adequate income, and this fact has been a blessing and a curse. This cliché is the only way I could think of to describe how I've always felt about my wealth. Believe me, I know, no one wants to hear that it is difficult to have money. Trying to write about it isn't easy, but I'm writing these stories for my three children, and I think they will understand.

In my early college years, I became a radical. To be truthful, a lot of my radicalization was more about finding a group of friends than my commitment to causes. I won't go into all my adventures as a revolutionary. I was never arrested, but I came close. My friends, when they realized I had money, wanted me to put my money where my mouth was. I had to face the fact that I didn't want to fund the revolution, and I fled to Northern California with Don Spillane.

Don provided me with an escape from my situation in San Diego. Now, I wasn't funding the revolution, but I was paying for my boyfriend's ambitions. I was with Don for about two years, and during that time, he purchased a business, and we purchased a house together. We got married. Then, we got divorced, which probably saved me from exhausting my entire trust fund. Don kept the house and his business. I remember talking to my older sister, Katie, at the time. She told me I would regret not fighting to get my money back from Don, but I just wanted out of my mistake, and I never looked back.

I was very lucky to meet Jim. He was interested in me not my money. We got married in Denver in my parents' elegant house. Jim's attitude toward money was just what I needed. He wasn't a miser, but he definitely hated to waste money. Throughout our marriage, his financial philosophy shaped our spending habits. Burney's Hot Dogs was Jim's business for the first twenty-three years of our marriage. He ran the small restaurant with great efficiency, and the money he made was great but not what paid all the bills. That is what was so different about our life. Jim could have a business he enjoyed, and he didn't have to worry about making enough money to support his wife and kids. I could be a-stay-at-home mom, and I could give them all the things they needed.

We didn't have the incredible stress that most young families face. So were we in the real world? For my entire life, I've tried to come to terms with that question.

Of course, I've always had the option to give away all my money or just not touch any of it and try to make it on my own. When I was in college, I knew a girl named Martha. She had the most beautiful long blond hair, which cascaded down her back. On one hellish road trip from San Diego up to Berkeley for an SDS conference, she was complaining about her beauty. Martha bemoaned the fact that she never knew if people only liked her for her looks. I felt like saying, "If you really feel that way, why don't you just cut your hair?" But I knew Martha would never cut her hair, and I know I will never give away all my money.

My relationship to "my moola" has mellowed through the years. Now, I'm even able to spend money on some extravagant things, like flying first class, without too much guilt. I'm grateful every day for the security and comfort the Shannon family money has given me. But I think I will always put an asterisk next to all my accomplishments—*done with the help of unearned income.

PAINTING SHOES

Katie's voice is filled with enthusiasm, "I think this could be really big. I saw them in the Neiman Marcus catalog going for one hundred and fifty dollars. They are painted Dr. Skolls wooden exercise sandals."

"Wait a minute", I'm thinking, "Dr. Skolls, isn't Skoll snuff or chewing tobacco?" I'm not sure, so I don't say anything.

My sister continues, "I went to a crafts boutique and a woman there was selling them for seventy-five dollars. They were nice, but I think with your artistic ability, we could really make some great shoes. I could take them to shops in Denver and Aspen and maybe you could paint some with horse themes and I could sell them at horse shows. (Katie's daughter, Shannon, is into showing) I'm going to mail you some shoes and painting materials and the photo from the catalog. This is going to be so great!"

I don't want to curb her enthusiasm, but I'm already having some reservations about this venture. After all, Katie and I were always dreaming about some sort of idea that would make money and give us a feeling of worth. Something we could say, "This is what we do. We paint and sell shoes."

Through the years we had had other possible business concepts- together and individually. These ideas were usually stopped in their tracks when we figured out they would require WORK. This shoe thing was going to be different though. Katie had the true enthusiasm and I was ready to buckle down and commit once and for all. Plus, I had just seen an Oprah program about ordinary women who became rich just acting on simple ideas...if they could do it, why not us?

A couple of days later a white box was delivered. I saw Katie's distinctive writing on the label and knew; the shoes had arrived. I put the unopened box in the dining room, no need to rush into anything here. The box sat on the dinner table. I was intimidated. Every time I thought about starting in on the project; something sidetracked me. Finally on Tuesday afternoon, I was out of excuses. I put the box on the kitchen table and opened it.

Inside the box I found: three pairs of Dr. Scholls (shoals) wooden sandals, a high-heeled pair of wood sandals and about on hundred dollars worth of paints and brushes. Katie was already heavily invested in the shoe business. Also enclosed was a small photo of three painted sandals from the Neiman Marcus catalog.

I was overwhelmed. Where should I start? I spread everything out on the kitchen table. OK, what could I paint on these shoes? I tried to hearken back to my art college days. Oh yeah, my famous sheep. I had done several prints consisting of a large primitively drawn sheep with many smaller sheep inside its' outline. Those little, tiny sheep would be perfect.

I thought the logical thing would be to make a pattern. I placed a sandal on a piece of paper and traced around the sole. Then I cut it out. I started drawing little sheep on the shoe pattern, then it kind of dawned on me; little, teeny tiny sheep would be pretty darn difficult to paint. Solution, I'd make the sheep bigger. I had a plan.

I picked up a sandal with a white strap. I decided I would paint the wooden sole red and then add the white sheep. I attempted to unbuckle the strap, so I could paint the sole more easily. I could not budge it. I pushed one way, then the other to no avail. A big screwdriver might help. I tried prying. "Be careful." I warned myself. (I had a long history of prying accidents.)

My husband, Jim, walked into the kitchen and asked, "What are you doing?"

"What does it look like I'm doing?" I snapped.

He picked up a sandal and tried the buckle. He couldn't budge it either. He looked in the shoebox and pulled out a small printed card, the directions. I read:

To open:

Slide buckle back. It slides more easily if you fold both sides of the wide bottom strap down with one hand and slide the buckle with the other.

WHAT? I still couldn't do it, grrrrrrr. Finally. I did get the darn thing apart. It was time to paint!

I squeezed a big red glob of red paint on a paper plate. With one of the brand new brushes I began applying the paint. Almost immediately I had problems. How was I going to avoid getting paint on the strap? Should I paint all the way down to the bottom of the shoe or just paint on the wood and stop at the top of the rubber sole? (Oh, I loved that album) I looked at the catalog photo again. It looked like the paint went all the way down.

Painting the shoe was hard. I started thinking, "If only I could spray paint the bottom, that would be much easier." It looked like the straps were held on with little gold screws. If I could remove the straps, the painting would go a lot faster. I took my big screwdriver and twisted the first little screw to the left, remembering, "righty-tighty, lefty-loosey." Whoops! The head of the screw broke off. Oh brother, I proceeded to the next screw, being careful not to use such brute strength. It came out OK and so did the next one. The strap didn't come off though, because it was also stapled down. So much for unscrewing the straps, I guess it's back to painting. Geez, I dripped paint on the bottom of the shoe, it smeared. I start thinking, "Maybe we could hire someone to paint the shoes." NO, NO, NO, this is supposed to be our own thing.

My son Jimmy walks into the kitchen. "Mom, when is dinner going to be ready?"

I look up at the clock, six o'clock already? Time flies when you're destroying shoes. I start clearing everything off the kitchen table. I need a studio. I need a worktable. I need to make dinner.

After dinner I get back to work. I paint little white blobs (sheep bodies) on the one red shoe. Now I need to let the paint dry and then I will paint a black outline around the white blob. Then I'll add four black legs, a little black head and Voila...a sheep! Waiting for paint to dry has never been my strong point. I can remember watercolor painting in Mrs. Moore's third grade class. I would paint a flesh colored head and invariably, when I went to add the eyes, nose and mouth, the paint would bleed into a muddy mess. Anyway, I'm grown up now. I can wait.

I decide to start in on another pair of shoes. I remember some paints I used on an earlier project. Where did I put that stuff? I find it under the sink in the bathroom of all places. There are two cans: dark green and navy blue. I look at the catalog photo again, this time with my reading glasses on. Oh no, the paint stops at the rubber sole line. I guess I screwed up that first red shoe.

I open the can of dark green paint. It is pretty runny and it takes all my concentration to brush it on the shoes. "American Idol" is on TV. I've been waiting all week to watch the show. Simon, the mean judge, tells Clay, "I liked your little move."

What move? I missed it. I was painting these stupid shoes. At ten o'clock I decide to call it a night. I have one red shoe with white blobs, two dark green shoes and two navy blue shoes. Not a very auspicious start, but at least I DID start. That's something.

Over the next few days I work on the shoes on and off. I discover I can't paint small delicate lines, no way. So, I start using acrylic paint markers. I have some good success with the markers. I decorate the dark green sandals with yellow flowers and the navy blue pair with spotted dogs. I paint the final pair of sandals white and add orange and hot pink flowers with the markers...very Vera. I also paint the final red shoe and add the white sheep.

I with all the materials Katie included a can of acrylic spray coating to protect the paint and add a shine. But how do you apply the stuff without getting it on the leather strap? I carefully cover the white leather straps on the two red sheep shoes with masking tape. This is not fun. I bring the sandals out on the deck and start to spray. Yikes, the black outline around the sheep is blurring and bleeding.

I have come to the realization…I could NEVER mass- produce painted shoes. I'll finish the four pairs and mail them back to Katie and then somehow I'll have to break it to her that the dream is dead.

Finally all the sandals are completed and from a distance, they do look pretty good. Just don't put on your reading glasses. I pack them back in the same box Katie used to mail them to me. I send them off, good riddance.

A few days later I get a call from Katie. "Trisha, I love the shoes. They're beautiful."

"Oh no," I think, now I'm going to have to tell her, "I DON'T WANT TO PAINT SHOES!"

But before I can say anything, she continues, "But I don't know about these Dr. Scholls exercise sandals. (now, she pronounces it correctly) I wore a pair last weekend and after a couple of hours I couldn't even walk. My feet and legs were killing me."

We talk a little longer, letting ourselves off the hook for not persevering and building a painted shoes empire. We'll never get on Oprah this way. Oh well, you know what they say, "There's no business like shoe business.

ROOKIE

I have been fortunate in my life to have loved and received the love of many people: my parents, my siblings, my children, and my wonderful husband, Jim. But the purest, most adoring love I have ever received was from a little dog named Rookie. Originally, the small dachshund puppy was supposed to be my daughter Meg's dog. However, as it often turns out with pets and children, I was the one taking care of the young dog, and she rewarded me with her complete loyalty.

I had never owned a small dog before. I was used to big friendly dogs, who gave their affection freely. Rookie was not like that. She was fiercely protective of the five of us and would have nothing to do with anyone not in our family. She barked and growled at all visitors, which was very embarrassing, but something we never were able to correct. This was not the only area of training in which we failed. I say "we" but it was actually "me." I really couldn't be strict with the little dog. I trained her to go to the bathroom on newspapers by rewarding her with small pieces of meat each time she peed or pooed on the paper. This toilet training was never adapted to having her go outside. As a result, she was really an indoor dog. I constructed a large box with low sides, which I lined with newspapers and paper towels, and for her entire, life a big part of her routine was going to the bathroom on the "pee pee place" and then getting a treat.

As a young dog, she was pretty playful. She liked to play tug of war with you, and she would toss her stuffed animals around. My son, Jimmy, loved having her chase him around the house, and he could really work her up into a frenzy.

Originally, she slept in the laundry room in a cozy bed we had made for her. One night though, she woke up and started crying. We let her out, and she came up on our bed. That one night is all it took, she refused to ever sleep in the laundry room again, and it was our bed from then on— another training battle lost.

Since Rookie was attached to our family and liked nobody else, it was hard for us to leave her with anyone when we went on trips. Over the years, we tried to find different solutions to this dilemma. We once boarded her at a veterinarian office in Colfax, and when we picked her up, they said they were sorry, but they could never board her again. For several years, Meg's friend, Jennifer, would dog sit for us. Jennifer was one of the few outsiders that Rookie would tolerate. More recently, I had a great woman in Meadow Vista, who would come in twice a day when we were gone. We never found the perfect solution to leaving our little dog. I always wished I could explain to her that we would be coming back when we went on a vacation. I felt so guilty leaving her because I knew she would miss the family and me in particular so terribly. When we did return from a trip, she would just go crazy with happiness, licking, wiggling, and jumping all over us.

As the kids grew up, went off to college, and eventually moved out, Rookie became more and more important in my life. She was my constant companion. I loved to have her sit on my lap while I watched TV in the evening. She would always come outside with me while I was gardening, and often while I was digging, she would also be busily digging right next to me.

Rookie was a pretty healthy little dog. Her reddish brown coat was always sleek and shinning. As she aged, she slowed down a bit and gained weight, but in December of 2005, at the age of twelve, she was still in fairly good shape. Rookie and I were outside, and I was working on our Christmas decorations. Our son, Rich, was home for winter break. He breezed out of the house and got in his Honda Civic, calling out that he was going to a friend's house. I don't know why I didn't take a hold of Rookie. I knew she always chased after any car that went down the driveway. I guess I figured she was too slow these days to catch up with the car, and I think Rich thought the same thing. Somehow though, she raced after the blue car and was run over. It all happened in a horrific instant. I ran to her as Rich jumped out of his car, shouting, "I'm sorry, Rookie, I'm sorry. Don't die, don't die." At that point, I was really more worried about Rich than I was about Rookie. I knew how terrible he felt.

Rookie was in so much pain. She was crying and when I first tried to pick her up, she snapped at me. I was able to pick her up though, and we got into Rich's car to drive to the vet's office. Fortunately, our vet was only minutes away. I tried to reassure Rich that I knew it was just an accident, and that Rookie would be OK.

When we got to the vet clinic, I quickly explained what had happened. A young vet tech. named, Christa, took Rookie from my arms and whisked her away. Dr. Pam came out and said that they would need to take x-rays and asked if I would authorize that procedure. For a brief moment, I considered saying that I felt it would be best to put Rookie to sleep, but then I realized Rich would be so crushed if she died. I felt she probably had severe internal injuries, but it seemed worth a try to keep her alive. The vet told us to go home and wait for her call. When I was back home, the reality of what it would mean to lose Rookie hit me hard. I didn't just want her to live for Rich's sake, I just desperately wanted her to live.

Dr. Pam called and said that miraculously Rookie had no broken bones or severe injuries. She said she wanted us to take her home, since she would be more comfortable there than at the clinic. I'll never forget bringing Rookie back to our house. She was all doped up and lay stoically on a blanket. That first night she really didn't move. She just lay on the blanket by our bed; it seemed as though she was in shock. I was getting worried because she hadn't had anything to eat or drink since the accident. In the morning, I gently lifted her to a standing position and placed her water bowl right next to her. She took a few licks of water. After that, I placed her on the pee pee place, where she took a few staggering steps and then peed. When I saw that, I knew she was going to make it.

I had loved Rookie before the accident, but after the ordeal, I loved her even more. I really admired the way she had bravely come through the whole thing. She made an amazing recovery and soon was doing most of the things she had done before. I began to spoil her shamelessly. I read the quote "food is not love" in a pet advice column. Logically, I knew that was true, but Rookie loved food, and I knew it made her happy. So although I knew that being fat was not good for her, I kept feeding her treats every time she went to the bathroom on the pee pee place and also at times when she would just bark persistently. I realized she needed more exercise, so I started walking her up and down our driveway on a leash. This was a somewhat tedious chore since she walked very slowly. However, the walks allowed me to really look around our yard and appreciate all the beauty of the trees.

Along with her added weight, Rookie had a lump in her chest, which spread to lumps around her neck. I was well aware of these growths, but I didn't take her to the vet. I made a conscious choice not to address this problem, and I knew it was partially because I really didn't want her to live an exceptionally long time. The problem of leaving her when we went on trips was a big part of my way of thinking. Now when we left Rookie to go on trips, she would become so upset that she contracted diarrhea. Obviously, this was not pleasant for anyone taking care of her. Part of me really wanted to be free to travel, without worrying about Rookie. Of course, if she had been in pain, I would definitely have had her treated, but she seemed to be doing OK. In fact, she was peeing and pooing with a regularity, of which I was envious.

This stage of Rookie's life was changed by a fall she had down the stairs. I witnessed the whole thing. She started down the stairs then, picked up speed, tumbled down the last four steps, and slid into the front door. She wasn't hurt, but the fall scared her. She was very reluctant to go down the stairs after that, and eventually, she wouldn't go down at all. Rookie would still go upstairs though, because she always wanted to sleep on our bed. When she wanted to come down, she would bark at the top of the stairs, and we would carry her down. Rookie, Jim, and I all adjusted to her new limited mobility.

Rookie continued to slow down in almost all areas. She would become winded with the least bit of exercise. I had to give up on our driveway walks. She no longer did that much barking when visitors came to the house, and she never did any digging when I took her outside. Her love of food never lagged though; in fact, it seemed to have intensified. In her entire life, I had always left a bowl of dry food for her in the laundry room, which she would nibble occasionally. Now, she was emptying the bowl every couple of days.

Every morning, it was the same routine. After we made the bed, Rookie would lie on her back on the bedspread and wriggle around. Jim and I would pat her and snuggle her. I loved to bury my face in her fat little neck. Then I would carry her downstairs and place her on the pee pee place. This started the peeing, pooing, barking, and begging cycle that lasted all through my breakfast hour. Jim called Rookie, "the queen of bodily functions," and she really did seem to be able to program herself to get the optimum number of treats. I had to clean the pee pee place more and more often. I even started having to go to the recycling bins to pick up extra newspapers. I didn't mind this chore. For me, cleaning the pee pee place was a labor of love.

Rookie slept most of the day. At dinnertime, we put her in Jimmy's room so she wouldn't bark at us the entire meal. In the evening, she would sit next to me on the sofa. Some nights, she would laboriously make her way upstairs on her own. But most nights, Jim would carry her up to our bedroom and gently tuck her under the tiger blanket on the bench at the end of our bed. I knew that she was deteriorating, but I wasn't sure how things were going to play out. At our Super Bowl party, one of our friends was talking about how recently her dog had been put to sleep. I told her I didn't think I would know when to make that decision with Rookie, and she said, "you'll know."

On February 10, 2007, our friends, John and Diana, invited us to go with them to a Valentine concert at Arco Arena called the "Love Jam." Going to that type of thing was unusual for us, but it turned out to be a fun evening. We got home very late, around 1:00 a.m., and when I went upstairs, I immediately saw that something was wrong with Rookie. The underside of her neck was severely swollen. I brought her downstairs. She peed and then waddled into the kitchen for a treat. With her swollen neck, she reminded me of the comics character, Fred Bassett. However, there was nothing comical about her situation. Rookie was breathing with difficulty. She looked at us with a sort of confused resignation. Jim carried her upstairs, and we went to bed. I could hear her labored breathing all night, and I didn't get much sleep. I thought seriously about what this new development meant.

In the morning, I carried Rookie downstairs, and amazingly, she went through her peeing and pooing routine. She ate her treats but didn't stand by the table barking at me as she usually did. She went into the living room and lay on the floor panting. I realized she was no longer able to bark.

I called our vet, but since it was Sunday, the answering service referred me to an emergency clinic in Roseville. I called down there and said we were bringing our dog in. I asked Jim if he would come with me and he said "of course." On the drive down, Rookie sat on my lap panting away, but she was very calm, not shaking as she usually did in the car. I told Jim I was considering euthanasia. He said, "Trish, she is your dog, and I'll support whatever you decide." I had decided, my friend was right, the time had come, and I knew it.

The Atlantic Street Veterinary Hospital was right off the freeway. It was a nice place designed to look like an old-time train depot. I was relieved to see there was no one in the waiting area. A young girl greeted us and took Rookie out of my arms, which I wasn't expecting. We filled out some paperwork and then the girl came back and asked if we would authorize x-rays for Rookie. I told her we were considering euthanasia. She left for a moment and then asked us to come into an examining room where we waited nervously. Then the vet came in. She was a young woman named Dr. Delaney. I looked her directly in the eye and said that we had decided that it would be best to put Rookie to sleep. She kindly said that she understood. She asked us if we would want to be with Rookie when it happened and we said "yes." She explained that a catheter would be placed in her back leg, and then when we were ready, the medicine would be administered. She suggested that we take care of the payment beforehand, so we could just leave afterwards. We were given a sheet of paper with the three options for taking care of the body. We chose to have her cremated, but we weren't interested in keeping her ashes.

Then we were led into another room, where there was an old sofa. Jim and I sat next to each other. We were both crying. We were given a blanket to put on our laps and then Rookie was brought in. The doctor said she would leave us alone and asked how long we would need to say "good bye." I answered it would only take a minute. Rookie was fighting for every breath and her eyes had a glazed look. I told her, "Thank you for all the love you gave me." The vet came back in and quietly placed the syringe into the catheter. The reaction was almost instantaneous. The life just seemed to flow out of Rookie, and she lay completely limp on our laps. She was gone. We were both really crying now and left the clinic in a blur of tears.

EPILOGUE

Jim and I are adjusting to life without our eccentric dachshund. I have almost enjoyed my sadness, just because it seems so pure. I realize how lucky I was to have been so completely loved by a little dog, named Rookie.

IT HAPPENED

It had been my idea to give my mom a fun time. Since my dad's death a few years earlier, she wasn't able to do many of the enjoyable things they had done together, like going on vacations and staying in beautiful hotels. Mom didn't like traveling alone, and because of my children, I wasn't able to go on many trips with her. I did manage to come back to Denver from California at least once a year. This time, I had made reservations at the old, historic Brown Palace Hotel. I had booked a two-room suite for one night. This was an extravagance my husband, Jim, would have thought of as "crazy," if we were going on a trip together. I had my own trust fund money, though, so I could do as I pleased when traveling alone.

The first couple of days of my visit, I stayed at my mom's house in suburban Denver. Then on Friday morning, we packed our overnight bags and got into mom's Buick. At the time, my mom was in her late seventies and was still a good driver. But for some reason when I visited her, I always drove her car. We headed for downtown Denver, taking Speer Boulevard, which ran along Cherry Creek. I enjoyed the drive, remembering all the times me and dad go this way to visit my grandmother Cather, who had lived in an apartment building called the Sherman Plaza. The colors were mostly brown and gray. That was Denver in early December.

When we entered the atrium lobby of the Brown Palace, it was like entering another world. Everyone seemed to speak in a hushed voice in deference to the beauty of the place. The floors were marble covered by rich old oriental rugs. The registration desk was along one wall and in the center of the lobby small tables were set up for afternoon tea. The ceiling went up to the top of the building and ended in an ornate stained-glass skylight. You could see each of the nine floors of the hotel surrounded by a gilded railing when you looked up. We followed the bellman into the old-fashioned elevator, which took us up to the third floor. When we entered the suite, Mom and I were both excited. It was like a beautiful little apartment with a living room, a kitchenette, and two bedrooms with their own baths. "Oh Trish," my mom exclaimed, "the suite is lovely." And even though we were only a few miles from my mom's house, I felt I had given her (just as I had wished) a small vacation.

At three o'clock, we went down to the lobby for afternoon tea, a tradition at the Brown Palace. It was the start of the holiday season, and there were red, green, and gold centerpieces on every table. My mom looked very pretty wearing a red wool blazer and a black pleated skirt. She was a small, feminine woman, and I always felt like a moose next her. An older waitress in a starched uniform served us a delicious array of finger sandwiches and pastries. I loved all the food, especially the chocolate confections. My mom insisted on paying the bill, even though I had told her repeatedly that I was paying for everything. We were heading back up to the suite, when Mom realized she hadn't picked up her credit card from the table. A look of worry and embarrassment crossed her face. I know she didn't like making a mistake in front of her daughter. That was just the way she was. Anyway, her card had been turned in at the front desk. So no harm was done.

That evening, we had dinner with my sister, Elizabeth, her grown daughter, Lisa, and Lisa's boyfriend, Mike. Mike was a nice man, but he was at least twenty years older than Lisa, which bothered me. We ate in the Ship's Tavern, a restaurant in the hotel. As the name suggested, it had a nautical theme. Polished brass lanterns hung from gleaming dark wood beams, and the tables were covered with red and white checked tablecloths. The meal went well, and though wine was consumed, no one got overly drunk, as was so often the case with my sister. After dinner, we all went up to the suite. We were surprised when we found a small platter of delicious desserts and a basket of fruits had been left in our kitchenette. I guess staying in a suite had its perks.

That night, there was a Christmas light parade in downtown Denver. The parade was a relatively new tradition for Denver, but it had already become a big deal. Elizabeth, Lisa, and Mike left to watch the parade. Mom and I opted to stay up in our little suite. I found that by looking out a small window in the back of the kitchenette, I could see parts of the lighted floats as they made their way down 16th Street. We watched a little TV together and then went to our separate bedrooms. I called home and talked to Jim. I told him that the trip was going great and that I missed him and the kids. I reminded him I would be home on Sunday.

Saturday morning, we both woke up and decided to take a short walk before we went to breakfast. It was clear and cold outside, and we basically just walked once around the outside of the hotel. Mom was a bit frail and couldn't walk too far. I had a disposable camera, and we each took a couple of photos of each other. We had breakfast in the beautiful hotel dining room. Sun streamed in the windows, and the white tablecloths looked elegant and especially white. We both ordered fresh-squeezed orange juice, dollar pancakes, bacon, and coffee—all my favorites. The waitress poured our coffee out of an elegant silver coffee pot. It was so rich and delicious. During the meal, I suddenly felt my nose began to run. I put my linen napkin up to my nostrils and was surprised and a little freaked out when I saw a bright red circle of blood on the cloth. I never had nosebleeds. My mom was concerned and told me to tilt my head up and pinch my nose. Fortunately, when I went to the ladies room, the flow stopped quickly. I carefully folded my napkin when we left the table, so the bloodstain didn't show.

We checked out of the hotel and waited on the sidewalk for the car to be brought around. The bellman put our two little overnight bags in the trunk, and we were off, with me driving. I decided to take a different way back to my mom's house, a decision I would later regret. First, I drove down to Larimer Street where Elizabeth's apartment was located and then I turned and headed toward City Park. We had just driven past old East High School, the school my dad had attended. The road we were on was a three-lane, one-way road, and I was probably going about thirty-five or forty-five miles per hour. All at once, I felt the car go sailing off to the left. Reflexively, I pushed my foot on the brake. The next thing I remember, the car was stopped, and I was pushed forward with my legs way under the steering wheel. I looked over to my mom. She was semiconscious and moaning.

Before I had time to think what I was going to do next, a man ran up to the side of the car and told me he had called the police. He asked me if I was all right. I said I was OK, but that my mother was hurt. I thanked him for calling the police. The police came almost immediately. I knew I had been in a car accident, but I wasn't sure if it was my fault. Maybe I went through a red light. I didn't know. I was still sitting in the driver's seat when an officer came up. He said he was going to ask me some questions but told me not to shake my head. The first thing he asked was, "Are you hurt?" I shook my head "no." He said, "I told you not to shake your head." Oh brother.

My mom started to come around, but she was hurt. I, of course, was wearing my seat belt, but my mom had not been wearing hers. She never wore her seatbelt, and I didn't make an issue of it, which obviously I should have. "Mom," I said, "we were in an accident."

Before I could say much more, the EMTs arrived. They opened the passenger door and started to examine Mom. Her right arm was scraped, and she had a cut on her head. I got out of the car and walked around to where the attendants were placing a stabilizing collar around my mom's neck. They gently helped her out of the car and on to a stretcher. It seemed like before I knew it, she was gone—off to the hospital.

A very nice female officer said she had to ask me some questions. I told her I wasn't sure what had happened, and I asked her if I had caused the accident. She then explained that a car driven by a sixteen-year-old boy had gone through a stop sign on a side street and hit the back of our car. I was so relieved that the crash hadn't been my fault. Just then, the driver of the other car came up to me and said he was sorry. I looked at him, and all I could think of was my son, Jimmy, who was also sixteen and was just starting to drive. What if this happened to him? I wanted to reassure this kid. I knew what a scary experience it must be for him. When I faced him though, I just started crying in little gasps and had to turn away.

The officer asked for my registration and proof of insurance. I explained it was my mom's car, so I wasn't sure where the papers were. I looked in the glove compartment, and fortunately, everything was there in an envelope. She then asked me if I knew of somewhere I would like the car towed.

I thought for a minute and gave the name of the dealership where my parents had purchased their cars for as long as I could remember. I then asked if I could go to the hospital to see my mom. She said she would drive me over there. Right before I got into the patrol car, I remembered our overnight bags were in the trunk. I told the officer I had some luggage in the trunk that I wanted to get out. I know she was wondering why we had suitcases. I couldn't really explain how we had been on an overnight holiday. How an outing that had been so much fun had turned into something awful and scary. I'd always known that bad things could happen and that life can change in an instant. But just as everyone always says, I didn't really think it could happen to me.

THE CENTURY PLANT

During my junior year in high school, I took botany. I learned about the century plant, a member of the agave family. The plant grows for several years and then shoots up a tall stalk covered with tiny new century plants. After that the plant dies. The process takes many years, though probably not as many as a hundred years. Anyway, the plant became known as the century plant. The existence of such an unusual botanical species intrigued me. At dinner, I brought up how neat I thought it would be to have a century plant that would last for my lifetime and then die about when I did.

At that time, my mom volunteered as a guide at the Denver Botanic Gardens, which housed many exotic tropical plants. To my surprise, she brought me home a tiny century plant taken from the giant one that grew under the multisectioned glass dome of the botanic gardens. My dad, a great gardener, planted the tiny little shoot in a small pot. That was the beginning of my century plant story.

For the next two years. I kept the little plant in my room. When I headed off to college in 1968, I entrusted the plant to my parents' care. I attended college in San Diego, where I discovered century plants grew in abundance. Each time I saw one, I would think of home.

In 1970, my parents sold their big, beautiful old house on Cedar Avenue, the house where I grew up. First, they moved to an apartment building, then to a condo, and finally in 1975 into an elegant house they had built for their "golden years." They took the steadily growing century plant on each of the moves.

Of course, during these years, I came back to Denver many times: first as a college student, then a radical college drop-out, then as a married woman, then a divorced woman, then a student again, and finally, as a remarried woman starting a family. The century plant by now had grown fairly large. My dad had replanted it many times. It was now in a big heavy earthenware container. We often discussed how I could take it back to California, but it always seemed like too much of a hassle.

In 1985, my wonderful dad died, and my mom started her life without him. She stayed on in their house, living with a strength and determination that amazed me.

My father had always been the undisputed head of the family. It seemed almost impossible that any of us could live without him, especially not my little mother. Mom did go on alone though, and some of those years after Dad's death were pretty good. My brother and two older sisters still lived in Denver, so she had family around her. I now had three children and a husband in Meadow Vista. I was tied down. I went back to Denver as often as I could, and Mom came out to California a couple of times. I called home once a week always on Tuesday night right after "Frasier," one of Mom's favorite TV shows. Nevertheless, I wasn't there "in the trenches" for my Mom's final years.

The last time I visited Mom was in March of 1995. She had been in the hospital with pneumonia but was now at home. She had to be on constant oxygen due to the diminished capacity of her lungs. Her house was rigged up with a machine, which pumped oxygen through a long, long plastic tube. The tube split into two smaller tubes, which went into Mom's nostrils and were held in place with an elastic band around her head. Mom also had a portable oxygen tank, she could use if she left the house. I wasn't prepared to see Mom so frail and sick, trailing a crazy long plastic tube as she shuffled around her beautiful home. Sure, I had seen elderly people in the supermarket with oxygen set-ups, but this was my mom.

I stayed with Mom just for four days, and during that time, my sisters, Katie and Elizabeth, and my brother, Rich, were trying to help Mom decide her future. It was decided that Mom would put her name on the waiting list of a very nice assisted care apartment house. In the meantime, an in-home health worker would come to the house every day to prepare a meal and look out for her. I knew that my mother didn't want to move and for that matter, didn't even like the idea of someone coming to the house. My mom didn't want to be a burden to her children, and apparently, we didn't want to be burdened.

So while some people care for their elderly parents for years, I took care of my dear little mother for a few days. She was very weak, but she somehow bathed herself and got dressed in the morning. She had so much stubborn dignity. I tried to take care of her the best that I could. I fixed her the tastiest meals I could think of, and her appetite was pretty good. We watched many hours of TV, and my mom napped frequently.

Mom's ankles were terribly swollen because her circulation was poor. Her skin was cracking because of the swelling, and I asked her if she would like me to rub lotion on her ankles. She said that would "be nice." Applying lotion to my mother's swollen feet and ankles is such a bittersweet memory for me. It was one of the few very small things Mom let me do for her. During the visit, we did a lot of reminiscing, and I tried in my own clumsy way to thank her for everything.

The morning I was going to leave to go back to California, Mom asked me, "Trish, what about your century plant?" She added, "I'm afraid I haven't been able to take very good care of it these last few years."

A wave of guilt washed over me. My mom was still taking care of me when I should be caring for her. "Don't worry, Mom," I said, "I'll think of something."

The century plant was in very poor shape. It snaked sideways out of its pot and was a sickly green. I thought I'd try to put it, roots and all, in a plastic bag and maybe transport it that way on the plane. But as I tried to take the plant out of the container, it broke and lay there pitifully. What a mess. Almost as an afterthought, I snipped the tip off the plant. I wrapped the little tip in a wet paper towel and put it in a ziplock sandwich bag, which I put in my suitcase. I cleaned up all evidence of the debacle. I didn't mention it to Mom; it was too sad.

Back in California, I put the little century plant tip in a jar of water on the kitchen windowsill. I talked to Mom frequently on the phone. Her voice was breathless and weak, but she was uncomplaining. A month after my visit, I got the telephone call from Katie telling me Mom had died. She wouldn't have to make that move to the assisted care apartment. She had died at night in her home.

Today, the century plant is on my kitchen windowsill. After I returned from Denver, the little tip sprouted roots in the water. Later, I transplanted it to a small pot. The succulent, green plant is small, but strong, just like my little mom, Margaret Cather Shannon.

SHE'S LEAVING HOME

Well, the day had finally come. The day my daughter, Meg, was leaving for college. All summer, I knew the day was coming. I constantly shared my feelings with my friends, telling them, "Oh, when Meg goes to school, I'm going to miss her so much." And I knew I was going to miss her terribly, more than I missed my older son, Jimmy, who had left home three years earlier to attend college in Wisconsin.

It doesn't sound right for a mother to say she will miss one child more than another. It's like saying that you love one child more than the other; but that's not it at all. The simple truth of the matter is, as the kids got older, I just spent more time with Meg than I did with my two sons. We had so much fun shopping and going to concerts together. I was going to miss those special times. But what I will miss most are the everyday activities: watching TV, talking in the kitchen and just being together. It sounds corny, but she understands "where I'm coming from." Meg appreciates who I am, and I treasure that feeling. So I will definitely miss Meg. At the same time, I want her to get out on her own, to become independent, and to have fun. At least, we will have the two days in the car on the drive to Walla Walla, Washington, to share together.

In my life, leaving for college was a traumatic and life-changing event. I recently wrote a story about it. After reading the story, Meg commented, "Mom, I'm not like you. I want to leave home. I want to go to college."

She's right, of course. She is a different person than I was at eighteen. Meg is more talented and self-confident than I ever was. She hasn't been as sheltered as I was growing up, but still, she is pretty innocent. Despite her bravado, I know she is somewhat nervous about starting school.

Meg's car is packed and ready to go. I got the car when my mom died a few years ago, and Meg has been driving it ever since. She has made the grandmotherly car her own by covering the back with bumper stickers and decals. This summer, she had a CD player installed using the money from her first job. I've made a pledge to myself that I won't criticize Meg's driving or complain about the music volume. I want this to be a mellow, special trip together.

And from the beginning, it is a special trip. Meg must have made her own private pledge to get along, because she drives carefully and keeps the music well below her usual listening level. The Buick is a comfortable car, and it almost seems to float down the road. Before long, we are past the airport exit on Interstate 5 North and heading on to places I haven't been before.

In three hours, we are passing Mt. Shasta and driving between magnificent crags. Why haven't I come here before? It's so close and so beautiful. I think to myself, Jim, Rich, and I should drive up here and spend the day sometime. I'm already trying to plan for life without Meg.

While Meg is driving, she reaches to adjust the bead choker she is wearing. The necklace breaks, and I help her take it off while she keeps her eyes on the road. I put the broken choker in the ashtray and say, "I'll buy you another necklace when I get back home. I'll mail it to you." I love buying things for Meg because she appreciates and accepts them.

We stop for lunch in Ashland, Oregon. It is a beautiful little town with colorful flower boxes along the sidewalks. We browse through a couple of shops, and I think to myself how much I'm going to miss shopping with Meg.

After lunch, Meg drives for a while, but she gets sleepy. So for the first time, I take the wheel. While she sleeps in the backseat, I think about Meg, and I wonder if she will like going to Whitman College. I hope with all my heart that she will.

Meg wakes up and climbs back into the front seat. We are making good time and will easily reach Portland before it gets dark. We don't talk much, but there is a good feeling between us. I check the map and see that we can take a turn off before we reach Portland that will cut over to 84 East, the highway to Walla Walla. I tell Meg I think that is the best way to go. She surprises me saying, "Mom, I want to see Portland and stay there. I thought we could go shopping in the morning. You said it is only a four-hour drive from Portland to Walla Walla, so we have lots of time."

She has a good point. I had been picturing just staying at a motel by the freeway, but my daughter's plan sounds like more fun. So we drive on to Portland and take the exit marked "Downtown."

Once in the city, things work out well. We spot a Hilton Hotel, and I run inside to see if we can get a room, while Meg waits in the car. We get a beautiful room and find a parking garage for the car. Finding good accommodations so easily makes me very happy. Nothing is going wrong. This is great!

It is a Wednesday night, and things are pretty quiet in downtown Portland. Meg and I stroll along the sidewalk appreciating the trees and sculptures that adorn the city. We check the menus of a few restaurants. Nothing strikes our fancy, so we decide to eat back at our hotel. It is a good decision. The food in the hotel dining room is outstanding. While we are eating, the final episode of *Survivor* comes on the television in the hotel bar. I change seats with Meg so I can't see the screen. For weeks, I have been wrapped up in the island "reality" show. I'm anxious to find out who will win the one million dollars, but I don't want my second-to-the-last night with Meg to be spent watching TV. Anyway, that's why they invented VCRs. Meg and I share a dessert. Three small scoops of sherbet: mango, raspberry, and orange drizzled with dark chocolate—delicious.

Once we are back up in the room, Meg asks if we can go over some questions about Tim O'Brien's book, *The Things They Carried*. Whitman mailed the book of Vietnam War stories to all incoming freshmen, along with a list of questions to be discussed the first week of school. We both read the book over the summer, and it is interesting to share our ideas. Meg is sharp, and I know she is going to do great at college.

Thursday morning, I wake up and think, "Today we will drive to Walla Walla. Our trip is almost over." For a couple of minutes, I want to close my eyes and escape the reality of that fact. But not really, of course not, I will "rise and shine" as my dad used to say. I quietly get out of bed and go into the bathroom. I take a shower and wash my hair. When I come out, Meg is awake. I flip on the television and find out that Richard Hatch is the winner of *Survivor*. I can't believe it. I thought for sure it would be Rudy.

I look out the window. Cool, gray clouds hang over the city. We get dressed, and I loan Meg a long-sleeved shirt so she won't get chilly. Down on the street, we walk around a couple of blocks. There is literally a coffee place on every corner. After stopping at Starbucks for a quick breakfast, we hit the stores, first Nordstrom. The clothes are beautiful, but the prices are outrageously expensive. Who has that kind of money?

Next, we enter a beautiful new downtown shopping mall. Now we could be "anywhere USA" the same stores, the same food places. This is American culture in the year 2000. The affluence never fails to amaze me. Meg and I have shopped like this so many times before, but today, our hearts aren't into the ritual. It is time to move on.

So after checking out of the hotel, we are back on the road. Meg is driving, and I'm trying to figure out the way to go. We get on the freeway OK, but we are in the wrong lane and miss the exit for I84 East. "Mom, why didn't you tell me to get over?" Meg demands.

"Well, you are the one who's driving. You should have read the signs yourself," I snap back. It is the first and only disagreement we have had on the trip. Meg takes the next exit and turns back. She gets on the right road this time, with no more problems.

In just a few minutes out of Portland, the scenery becomes dramatically beautiful. The wide, dark Columbia River is to the left, and on the right, steep, rocky cliffs rise up out of brilliant green rain forests. Again I think to myself, "Jim and Rich should see this."

As we drive east, the landscape quickly changes. Brown rolling hills replace the lush vegetation. The road still follows the wide Columbia. Meg and I listen to a John Lennon CD.

The drive goes by quickly, and after only a few hours, we reach the turn off for Wall Walla, the little town where Whitman College is located. Our trip is almost over. For the first time during the whole drive, we run into road construction and are stopped by a flagman. I don't mind the delay. I don't really want the drive to end.

Once in Walla Walla, we easily find the Howard Johnsons Motel where we will both stay tonight and where I will stay alone on Friday night after Meg moves into the dorm. Now the weather is hot, and the motel air conditioner wheezes away. We lie on our beds watching an old episode of *Beverly Hills 90210* on the small TV.

We decide to walk to "downtown" Walla Walla for dinner. The town is small, and it is a short walk. Meg and I eat at a little Italian restaurant. An Asian family—mom, dad, and son—sit at another table. The son is undoubtedly an incoming Whitman freshman like my daughter. I almost feel like we should go over to their table and introduce ourselves. It is too soon to make contact though. We will wait until the official orientation tomorrow.

After dinner I ask Meg if she wants to walk around the campus and check out her dorm building. She says, "No." She wants to go back to the motel. So we split up for a while, and I walk around the campus by myself. The sun is low in the sky and the beautiful, big old college trees cast long shadows across the lawns. I find Meg's dorm, Anderson Hall, an attractive three-story brick building. I can imagine my daughter living here. Last spring, when we visited Whitman, I thought it was it was a beautiful school. Now on this late summer evening, the campus is even better than I remembered.

When I get back to the motel, Meg is sort of subdued. I can tell she is thinking about tomorrow. I tell her I looked at her dorm, and it seems really nice. She asks, "Mom, what if I don't like my roommate?"

Meg already knows her roommate's name is Juli Armstrong. She has looked up her picture in the campus directory the school mailed out. In the photo Juli looks like a blond, popular cheerleader, not really Meg's type.

I don't know what to tell Meg, so I state the mom's mantra, "Everything will be OK." And again, I hope to myself that everything will be OK and that my daughter will like college.

Meg is a very creative person. She has many talents. Perhaps the most impressive is her drawing ability. But she also has a flair for: fashion design (her clothes), interior design (her room), and sculpture (the many neat objects she has created like an umbrella made out of foil gum wrappers). Lots of times when she was bored over the summer, she would do some kind of art project. Recently, she made a chess set by painting some old plastic toy animals. She brought the painted pieces and board with her, and now she asks me, "Mom, do you want to play a game of chess?"

I don't know how to play chess. Heck, I'm not even good at checkers. But I can see Meg is trying to find a way to take her mind off all the uncertainties of tomorrow. So I agree to a game. Meg sets up the board with the red and green painted giraffes, elephants, rhinos, and various farm animals, and we pass our last night together playing an odd version of the game of chess. I'm glad we didn't just watch TV.

The next morning, we wake up, and I ask Meg if she wants to go to the complimentary breakfast served downstairs. She says she is too nervous to eat. So I make coffee with the little in-room coffeemaker and eat a bagel we brought with us. I'm rarely too nervous to eat.

Meg puts on a longish black skirt and I ask, "Do you really want to wear that?" I'm thinking it will be hot and uncomfortable. Or maybe I'm just trying to exert my last little bit of control.

Meg sticks with the skirt, and we get in the car and make the very short drive over to the school. I scoped out the parking lot last night on my walk, so I know right where to direct Meg to go. All around us are kids and their parents carrying boxes, suitcases, and computers.

We enter Anderson Hall and go to the registration table. Meg states her name, and the friendly girl says, "Oh, Meg, you are in my section." She hands her a set of keys and tells her the room number. We walk up the one flight of stairs and down the hall to room E-206. This is it.

Meg's roommate and her mom are already in the room. For me, there is an immediate sense of relief. Juli isn't a lot's of make-up cheerleader type. She is an outdoorsy, athletic, open type. I like her right off the bat, and I like her mom, Moriah, too.

The four of us start getting acquainted. Juli and Meg are hitting it off well. They easily decide who will have which bed, desk and closet. Meg and I begin carrying her stuff up from the car. She sets up her CD player and she and Juli start comparing their musical tastes. They like some of the same music. This is good. This is really good.

Juli and her mom need to go into town to set up a checking account. We agree to get back together for lunch. Meg and I start putting her stuff in the drawers and closet. I can see Meg is happy. In fact, she is glowing. From another room, Meg hears the strains of a certain song. She rushes down the hall to see who shares her affinity for the musician, Beck. Meg brings two girls back with her, and the room is filled with their excited chatter. One of the girls tells Meg, "I love your skirt."

Meg shows them a drawing she has done of Beck. One of the girls, Andrea from Minnesota, runs to her room and brings back a painting she has done of a snowboarder. I just sit back and observe. I see my daughter with her beautiful smile and her open friendly personality, and I know she is going to be all right at college.

When Juli and her mom get back, we walk over to Clarettes, a little coffee shop right off campus. We invite Andrea to come with us. I marvel at all three girls as they talk about their sports experiences and summer jobs. They communicate so well. No one tries to dominate the conversation or show the others up. Moriah and I glance at each other and smile. We are proud of our daughters.

That afternoon I attend a meeting for the parents. There are various speakers: deans, professors, and counselors. The organization and sincerity of their talks impresses me. I'm especially touched by the comments of a kindly looking counselor. He says, "Your children will change. When they come home, they will be different." I know this is true. I know Meg is leaving home and leaving childhood behind. I know college will change her. But I also know the love we have shared for so many years will never change.

The rest of the orientation is uneventful but good. All the activities the school has planned are geared to helping students and parents make the transition and they really do help. That night, I sleep alone at the motel. I try to imagine how Meg is doing in her dorm room. I'm worried that she is hot, since there is no air conditioning in her building. I feel guilty that I have AC, and she doesn't.

The next morning, there is a convocation ceremony. Most of the students look a little bleary-eyed. Meg looks good though, and it makes me happy that she sits next to me during the ceremony. Some of the kids are already pulling away from their parents.

Now it is time for me to go home. Meg will be keeping her car at school, so I am flying back home. When Meg takes me to the little Walla Walla airport, we say "good bye" but we don't cry. She has to get back for a meeting at her dorm, so I just get out of the car. I say, "I love you, Meg. Have fun."

Meg said, "I love you too, Mom. Thanks for driving up here with me and for everything."

I watch her drive away. I turn and enter the little airport. I'm going home to Jim, Rich, and our little dachshund, Rookie.

So that is the "taking-my-daughter-to-college story." It has been almost two months now since Meg has been gone. Every time she calls from

Whitman, she sounds happy and excited. Meg still gets along well with Juli, and she has made some really good friends. They are not any of the girls I met, but some kids from the Drama Department, go figure. As I expected, I miss Meg. I write her short letters and send her small gifts and that seems to help. I remembered to mail her a bead necklace like the one that broke on the drive up to Walla Walla. Last week, Meg sent me a Whitman tee shirt. And when I wear it, I feel she is close to my heart.

VISITING OLIVIA

She wasn't my mom, she was my friend Pam's mom. I visited her to be nice, to do something good. Originally, I had invited her out to lunch. We went to a few different restaurants, but it was so hard helping her in and out of the car. Also, she was a very picky person, and the way she treated the waitresses really embarrassed me. So I decided that instead of taking her out, I would just visit her in her apartment. Olivia seemed to be fine with that decision.

Olivia lived in a big three-story assisted living apartment building. The place was really nice, not depressing, at least not too depressing. You entered the building through the big open, airy lobby. There were several nice sofas placed around, and a big brass chandelier hung down in the middle of the atrium. Usually, there were a few residents sitting in the lobby. I always said "good morning" in a cheery voice as I walked by them on my way to the sweeping staircase up to the second floor.

A smell of coffee, cleaning products, and old people always hung in the air. The first time I visited Olivia, I walked down the carpeted hallway to her apartment with a lot of nervousness. I had called her the day before to set up the visit, but what if she had forgotten? Or, what if she was still in her nightgown? She wasn't in the best of shape after all. I knocked on her door, tap tap tap a tap tap . . . tap! tap! I tried to make my knock sound upbeat. It took a little while, but Olivia came to the door. She was a small, thin woman, and though she was eighty something, her hair was brown not gray. She was dressed very nicely. I guess my worries were unfounded.

Her apartment was basically one room. As you entered, a refrigerator, sink, and stove were to your right. On the left was an antique break front loaded down with clutter: tarnished silver pieces, mail, pills, and candy wrappers. From this entry area, the room opened up into the living room slash, bedroom. A blue fabric sofa faced the TV or should I say TVs, because there was a newer TV sitting on top of an old console model television. A nice wingback chair, covered with clothes, was to the left of the sofa. I was disturbed to see a yellowish Depend diaper resting on the arm of the chair. The room was warm, and the smell of urine was strong but not unbearable.

We both sat down on the sofa, Olivia in what I would learn was her regular spot. I sat at the other end at an awkward angle facing her. I handed her the *Good Housekeeping* and *Woman's Day* magazines I had purchased for her. She thanked me. "What are we going to talk about?" I wondered.

I didn't have to wonder long, because Olivia started right in, "Trish, you wouldn't believe the horrible food they have here. It is just awful. Last night, they served broccoli soup. Have you ever heard of broccoli soup? Well, I hope you never have to eat it. What I wouldn't give to have some smoked ham or some crab cakes. When I was growing up in Virginia, my father was a doctor. He drove all over the county, and I went with him."

Once in a while, I would interject a "that's interesting" or "you don't say?" After about forty-five minutes of listening to her nonstop monologue, I said I would have to get going. I asked her if there was anything I could do before I left. She said it would be nice if I took out the trash. There was a big plastic wastebasket in the entry way and a smaller one in her little bathroom. Both were crammed with Depend diapers. I discreetly plucked the diaper off the chair and disposed of it also. Once I had the contents of both baskets bagged up, I asked Olivia, "Where should I take these?" Luckily, Olivia's apartment was right next to the laundry room, where there was a big trash tote. I stuffed the bags in the tote. I was never sure how the other residents felt about Olivia's smelly trash.

I got into a routine of visiting Olivia once a week. It wasn't *Tuesdays with Morrie* by any means. I soon figured out she preferred *The National*

Enquirer or the *Star* to the women's magazines I had originally brought her. She knew everything there was to know about Princess Diana, Oprah, and Michael Jackson. I learned a lot about them too. I also learned what it was like to be old.

The Oaks, where Olivia lived, was really a nice facility from what I could tell. Meals were served in the formal dining room three times a day, and there were activities going on all the time. But there was such a wide range in the condition of the residents. Some were in very good health and still driving. Others, like Olivia, weren't able to do much. I had always thought if you were in a nice assisted living facility when you go old that you would have it made. I figured that you would be around other people and wouldn't be lonely. That really wasn't the case though. I began to realize that there was a hierarchy at the Oaks and that Olivia, because of her deteriorating health and messy apartment, was becoming an outcast. In a way, it wasn't that much different from high school, with the cool kids and the not-so-cool kids.

My visits with Olivia continued. She was not longer dressed up when I came, and sometimes was even in her nightgown. On one particular visit, she answered the door without her false teeth. Her face was sunken in, like a hillbilly woman. I was shocked at how old she looked. Olivia explained that her dentures were really bothering her and asked if I minded that she wasn't wearing them. Of course, I assured her it was OK. Her feet were also very painful, and she had a lot of difficulty walking even with her walker. When we were settled on the sofa, she didn't wait for the usual exchange of pleasantries, but launched into a long dialogue.

"Trish, you wouldn't believe what happened last night at dinner. When I went to sit at my usual table, there was a new woman in my chair. I asked her to move, but then Jeanne and Betty told me to find another seat. I've been sitting at their table for almost three years, listening to all their same old stories, and they have the nerve to tell me where I can sit. Don't they know that when I was a little girl growing up in Virginia, my father was a doctor? He went all over the county on his rounds, and I went with him."

I tried to interject a few words of sympathy, but Olivia wasn't really listening to me. She just continued with her same old stories. Before I left, I took out the trash and tried to straighten the apartment up a little bit. As I walked to my car, I was feeling so depressed, thinking about Olivia's situation. I wished I had never started visiting her. She had a family after all. She was their problem, not mine. Instead of feeling good about "brightening" an elderly woman's day, I was being brought down by the whole thing. When I'd wake up in the morning and it was hard to get out of bed, I would wonder what it must be like for Olivia to get up in the morning. How did she manage it? And then, the most frightening thought would come into my mind, "What will it be like for me when I get old?"

The next time I called Olivia and asked her as I always did, "Would you like me to come for a visit tomorrow at ten?" She hesitated.

"Trish, I don't know if you should come. I was sick last night, and I couldn't get to the bathroom. My carpet is all soiled."

"Oh, don't worry about it," I replied gamely, "I'll bring some carpet cleaner and take care of it."

So armed with my rubber gloves, a can of spray carpet shampoo, and a roll of paper towels, I knocked on Olivia's door the next day. It took her a long time to answer the door. She had an attitude of defeat about her. "Oh, Trish, I'm ashamed to have you come in. There's diarrhea all over the carpet."

I tried to make light of the situation, "Olivia, don't worry about it. I'll get it cleaned up."

I followed her into the apartment and immediately saw what she was talking about. A semicircle of brown stains dotted the carpet around her bed. I steeled myself, forced down my gag reflex, and got to work. I was able to get most of the mess up, but there were still light brown stains on the mauve carpet and a sour smell hung in the air.

For once, Olivia wasn't in the mood to talk. She sat in her usual spot with her head down. After I was finished and had taken out the trash, I asked her, "Are you OK?"

Olivia turned to me and said, "I want to thank you for visiting me. You don't know how much it has meant to me to have a friend."

"Oh, Olivia," I said, "I love you." And to my surprise, I did love her. She might not be one of those wise, dignified senior citizens, but she was a survivor. And she kept living, even though living wasn't any fun.

It wasn't long after that visit that Olivia was asked to leave the Oaks. Pam, her long-suffering daughter, arranged to have her moved to another assisted living facility, Foothills Oaks. It was a step down from the Oaks, but still nice. Her first night there, she fell out of bed and was taken to the hospital. After that, she was moved to a nursing home. I continued to visit her at the Sierra Oaks Nursing Home. She was now in a place where she was getting the care she needed. She was safe and clean, but it hardly mattered, because Olivia really wasn't there anymore. She could no longer walk and was usually in bed when I came to see her. She still recognized me but didn't do much talking. I guess the best way to describe her would be apathetic. At Sierra Oaks, she no longer was the person in the worst shape; in the nursing home, everyone was in pretty bad shape.

The last time I saw Olivia was right after I had been back to Denver for my brother's funeral. He had died a few months before his sixty-first birthday. I realized he would never experience the indignities of old age that Olivia was going through. I couldn't help but think, maybe it was better that way.

When Pam phoned me to tell me that her mother had died in her sleep the night before, I wasn't surprised. I told her I was so sorry. But I had to admit to myself, I was relieved. There would be no more visits to the nursing home, no more facing the realities of old age.

Christmas Letters and Poems

Christmas has always meant a lot to me. When I was little, I imagined the calendar year as being a round globe. You had to travel around the whole world in twelve long months until you reached the top, the best time of the year—golden Christmas! I was one of those lucky little kids whose parents loved Christmas. They did everything they could to make the holiday special for their children. Those childhood Christmases were so magical, that it was hard for me when I reached my late teens and early twenties, and Christmas lost its luster. But then when Jim and I started our own family, the magic returned.

We came up with our own family traditions. One of those was to take a family photo each year and send out photo Christmas cards. Later on, I added a holiday letter, and then in 2003, I wrote the first Schreiber family poem. What follows here are those letters and poems.

Schreiber Holiday Letter, 1998

Greetings! Family and Friends,

I hope the season finds you happy and healthy. For our family, 1998 was really great. As you can see by the photo, the kids are growing up, and Jim and I are as young as ever (ha ha). We took this photograph right before Jimmy left for college, and as I write this letter, I'm getting so excited to think he will be home in a couple of weeks.

Jimmy is in his second year at St. Norbert College in De Pere, Wisconsin. He is majoring in art and doing well in his classes. He is also working at the student union and was promoted to manager this year. Jimmy really seems to love Wisconsin. It must be the cheese.

Meg just turned seventeen and is a junior in high school. She has a heavy load of classes this year, but she seems to be able to handle all the homework, and her grades are great. She is still playing soccer and is a fullback on the school team. For fun she draws, listens to music and hangs out with her friends. She is still a big Beatles fan, yeah, yeah, yeah.

Rich is in eighth grade. His favorite class is journalism, and he has written some excellent articles for the *Warrior Times*. He is the copy editor for the paper, and he seems to enjoy picking apart his classmates' work. His soccer team is wrapping up a good season and going to District Cup. Rich is also on the school basketball team, and their games will start after the first of the year. Rich is a dedicated student, but he also finds time to flip through the channels, play video games, and talk on the phone.

Jim is still selling the best hot dogs in Auburn. He is also putting in many hours of volunteer work as president of the Forty-Niner Youth Soccer League. To stay in shape, he rides his bike to work, runs, and plays golf. He is still brewing beer and has had some great batches—Cheers!

Finally, I continue to teach step and aerobics which I really enjoy. I also teach water aerobics three times a week, which I love (except when the chlorine level was super strong). This year, I grew a bumper crop of pumpkins and sunflowers. I've read about twenty books on mountain climbing throughout the year. I've really enjoyed the armchair adventures.

It's hard to try to convey your life in a letter. I guess the bottom line is our family is happy and healthy and for that we are very grateful.

THE SCHREIBER FAMILY CHRISTMAS PICTURE 1999

"Come on you guys, it's time to take the picture for this year's Christmas card," I yelled as I stomped around the house. It was a beautiful, warm

Sunday in July. I knew from past experience how hard it was to get everyone together for the photograph, so this year, I was determined to get a jump on the process.

I knocked on Meg's bedroom door. "Come in," she hollered over the drone of Bob Dylan's voice. I opened the door. Meg was sitting on her bed sketching on a large pad. At seventeen, Meg is a very good artist. "Mom, why do we always have to take the picture when my face is broken out?"

"Oh," I replied, "Meg, you look fine. You're beautiful."

Next, I found Jimmy sitting at the computer. He was home for the summer having completed his second successful year at St. Norbert College in Wisconsin. "Jimmy, we're going to take the family picture now."

"Mom, don't you think we are getting a little old for this picture thing?" he grumbled.

"It's a tradition." I countered. "We haven't missed a Christmas in the twenty years since you were born."

He smiled, "Oh, OK, I'll be ready in a few minutes.'"

Fourteen-year old Rich was outside shooting baskets. I watched, impressed as he drained shots from all over the court into the net. "Hey, Rich, come on, we're going to take our Christmas picture right now."

He called back, "Now, Mom? I'm all sweaty."

Back inside, I approached Jim. He was working on the Sunday crossword puzzle. "I think I've got the kids ready for the picture. Remember I told you yesterday I wanted you to take it today?" I nagged.

"You did?"

"I did."

"Are you sure?"

"I'm sure."

"I'll have to check and see if I have some film."

"Jim, you make me so mad."

Ten minutes later, the family is all assembled in the yard. Jim patiently sets up the camera, and the kids horse around with each other. Our little dachshund, Rookie, happily sniffs the ground. I pick her up, so she will be in the picture. We gather in close. Jim sets the timer on the camera and runs quickly to kneel in his spot down in front. CLICK.

Merry Christmas to all and on to the year 2000!

SCHREIBER FAMILY FAST FACTS 2000

JIMMY, AGE 21

On track to graduate from St. Norbert College in Wisconsin on May 20th, 2001—Plans to work as a graphic artist or return to school to obtain a teaching credential.

MEG, AGE 19

Attending Whitman College in Walla Walla, Washington—Plans to attend Whitman for the next three and a half years.

RICH, AGE 15

A sophomore at Colfax High School, playing soccer and basketball and studying hard—Plans to get his California driver's license and become a pro wrestler with the WWF.

TRISH, AGE THE BIG FIVE 0

Still teaching step, aerobics and water aerobics—Still buying mass quantities of food at the supermarket (even though there is only one kid still at home)—Plans to keep teaching as long as the old body holds up.

JIM, AGE 51

Selling Burneys Hot Dogs after 22 years in business—Still golfing, riding his bike and running—Plans to referee basketball, work on the house, visit his mom in Chicago, enjoy life!

ROOKIE, AGE 7

Still baking at anyone who comes over—Plans to continue to protect the Schreiber Family with all her Dachshund strength.

MERRY CHRISTMAS AND HAPPY NEW YEAR

SCHREIBER FAMILY UPDATE 2001

Jimmy, Age 22

Jimmy graduated from St. Norbert College last May. He is now living in Madison, Wisconsin, working for an after-school program, teaching kids art. He got a new Honda Civic at the beginning of the summer, and he has put many miles on the little car driving to Chicago to see his relatives and to De Pere to see his girlfriend, Becky.

Meg, Age 20

Meg is a sophomore at Whitman College in Walla Walla, Washington. Last summer, she took an art class through Colorado College (3 weeks in Colorado Springs and 6 weeks in Paris) Next Fall she plans to transfer to another college??? that is stronger in art. Meg is really studying hard and doing some great painting. She is a serious student, but she still manages to have fun.

Rich, Age 16

Rich got his driver's license last June, so he drives up to Colfax High School every day, where he is a hardworking junior. He played sweeper on the varsity soccer team, which won the section championship this fall. Right now, he is starting basketball and in the spring, will play tennis or golf. He has put on several wrestling shows in our backyard ring: "The Heat Wave" and "The Fall Brawl" to name a couple. (I know what you are thinking, but the kid has to have a hobby.)

Trish and Jim, Combined Age 103

Jim and I are doing great. We celebrated our 25th wedding anniversary in November. We are both adjusting well to our post-Burneys lifestyle. Jim has been refereeing soccer and basketball games. He still runs and rides his bike. This holiday season he is volunteering as a Bell Ringer for the Salvation Army. I'm still teaching water aerobics, which I love.

After September 11th, we have appreciated each other even more than before. On November 24th, we watched the Leonid meteor shower together. It was an awesome event with about twenty shooting stars a minute at one point. Looking up at the stars, we were so thankful to be alive and have our wonderful family.

MERRY CHRISTMAS, HAPPY NEW YEAR

PS: Rookie is alive and well and still as obnoxious as ever.

SCHREIBER FAMILY CHRISTMAS LETTER 2002

Hello family and friends! This year, we are each writing our own paragraph to let you know "what's happening."

TRISH

I don't have much new news to report. I'm still teaching water aerobics, which I love for two reasons: the exercise and my great students. I guess the biggest event of my year was participating in the Avon 3 Day Breast Cancer Walk in July. I was on a team, the Sierra Sole Sisters, with five wonderful friends. We walked from San Jose to San Francisco, spending two nights in tents. It was a cool experience I will never forget. Oh, I also grew a ton of gourds.

JIM

If you think it is painful reading the Christmas letters, you ought to try writing one, so let's make it easy for all of us and just leave at MERRRY CHRISTMAS!!!!!

JIMMY

Greetings from California! I'm currently living back in Meadow Vista, something I vowed never to do after high school. The past couple months have been a struggle to determine the next step in my life. I've finally decided that I am going to start my own business online designing T-shirts. Of course, I can't be certain that it will be successful. I won't know until I try. Happy Holidays!!!!

MEG

Life is pretty wonderful. Over the past semester I have been living with my best friend in Tempe, AZ, and attending Arizona State University. Although I enjoyed my time at Whitman College, ASU has been a very positive change for me. I am eventually going to graduate with a BFA in painting, but over the past semester I have had the opportunity to take a number of interesting courses outside of my major. Some of these include: German, Astronomy, and Contemporary Women's Studies. At the beginning of next semester I am going to Regensburg, Germany, through an ASU language program. Then later in the summer, I will be coming back to Chicago to take classes at the School of the Art Institute.

I have a lot of good times ahead of me and a lot of great people to share them with.

RICH

I'm enjoying my senior year of high school. I played soccer in the fall and now I'm playing basketball. In the spring, it will be tennis. What can I say? I like sports. I've applied to several colleges. I'll let you know next Christmas which one I ended up attending. Have a good Christmas.

ROOKIE WOOF!

In 2003, I started the tradition of writing a Christmas poem instead of a letter. I know nothing about writing poetry, so I just tried to string some rhyming phrases together.

SCHREIBER CHRISTMAS RHYME, 2003

Just for fun, I thought I'd try
To rhyme the news of the year gone by.

James or Jimmy, our oldest son,
Has been spreading his wings and having some fun.
In early September off to Prague he flew
To have an adventure and experience something new.
The Czech Republic, Slovakia, Germany, and Poland,
From hostel to hostel he just kept on rolling.
Recently, he has been in Amsterdam, Rotterdam, Antwerp, and Ghent.
We keep track of his travels by the e-mails he's sent.
He's coming back home on the 13th of December.
He says this has been a trip he will always remember.

Meg is living in Flagstaff and attending NAU.
She's painting and drawing and printmaking too.
Her apartment is a dump, but it is close to the school.
She has lots of roommates and friends, and they're all pretty cool.

Rich is at the University of Washington in his first term.
He's still working his muscles and keeping them firm.
He pledged Sigma Chi at the very last minute,
After seeing his dorm room, he didn't want to stay in it.

Jim is delivering "meals on wheels," golfing, gardening, refereeing
Soccer and biking
All the activities listed above are things to his liking.

As for me, Trish, I'm enjoying my life,
Teaching water aerobics and being Jim's wife.
TO ALL OUR FAMILY AND FRIENDS
WE WISH YOU GOOD CHEER
MERRY CHRISTMAS TO YOU AND A HAPPY NEW YEAR!

SCHREIBER CHRISTMAS POEM

2004

AS THE YEAR 2004 DRAWS TO A CLOSE
I DECIDED TO WRITE A POEM INSTEAD OF SOME
PROSE

TO LET OUR FAMILY AND FRIENDS KNOW WHAT IS UP
WITH OUR CREW
I'LL TRY TO GIVE THE FACTS AND RHYME THEM TOO

JAMES, OR JIMMY AS WE CALL HIM, IS 25 YEARS OLD
HE LIVED IN AUBURN FOR THE LAST YEAR AND IN
NOVEMBER HIT THE ROAD
IN HIS LITTLE BLACK HONDA HE IS DRIVING STATE BY
STATE
HIS FINAL DESTINATION IS IN THE HANDS OF FATE

MEG, 23, WILL GRADUATE FROM NAU IN THE SPRING
SHE LOVES LIVING IN FLAGSTAFF AND ART IS HER
THING

RICH IS 19 NOW AND HE TRANSFERRED TO THE
UNIVERSITY OF SANTA CLARA
HE IS ALSO WORKING AT EXPRESS AND HELPING
CUSTOMERS DECIDE WHAT TO WEAR-A

AS FOR ME AND JIM, I'M THANKFUL TO SAY,
WE ARE HEALTHY AND HAPPY AND ENJOYING EACH
DAY

IN CLOSING, I WOULD LIKE TO WISH YOU GOOD CHEER
I HOPE 2005 IS A WONDERFUL YEAR!

Schreiber Family Poem

2005

Jim and I are home alone.
One by one, the kids have grown.
And though we miss or beloved three,
We still have each other and little Rookie.

Jimmy, our oldest is living in the Midwest.
Madison or Chicago? He's deciding which one is best.

Meg is busy preparing for her Senior Art Show.
It is down in Flagstaff, and we are definitely going to go.

Rich is still attending Santa Clara and working at Express.
He has his own apartment and we see him a lot less.

Jim is reffing, golfing, biking, and such.
He grows great vegetables, which we enjoy so much.

I'm really loving teaching my water aerobics classes.
And I'm reading a lot of books, wearing my glasses.

Every year, it is so important to me,
To keep communicating with my friends and family.
So with all my heart, I wish you good cheer!

HAVE A MERRY CHRISTMAS
AND
A HAPPY NEW YEAR!

SCHREILBER CHRISTMAS POEM, 2006

It is time again to compose the Holiday Verse
I'll try to do better than last year,
Or at least not any worse

Jimmy is happily living in the "windy city"
He is working for an events planner
Making the tables look pretty
He is also taking some computer classes online
When these are completed,
He should have a career that is fine

In October, Meg decided to make a major move
She went to New York to get into a new groove
She's working in a ceramics studio
Called the Painted Pot
Her apartment is in Brooklyn
And she likes it a lot

Rich will graduate from Santa Clara University next May
This Christmas, he had a great opportunity
To get away
He is flying to China with a good friend
Traveling for him is becoming a trend
Last summer, he went to Germany to see the World Cup of soccer
He had great stories to tell, he's a very good talker

Jim and I are doing quite well
We took a trip to New York that was really swell
At the Tavern on the Green with our kids by our side
We celebrated thirty years of marriage
It has been a great ride

This Christmas season, we'll miss the loved ones who are no longer here
But we are thankful for all we have and we will be of good cheer
To all of you, family and friends receiving this card
Merry Christmas, Happy New Year, and don't work too hard!

SCHREIBER CHRISTMAS POEM, 2007

As the year two thousand seven ends
It is time to connect with family and friends

Our family is spread far and away
James in Chicago
Meg in Athens, Georgia
And Rich in San Jose

All three kids are out of college these days
They are showing their creativity in many different ways

James is designing websites with technical skill
And working for an events company, which is a thrill

Meg is writing *Oh Hey*, an illustrated book
On her blog, www.ohheymeg.blogspot.com, you can take a look

Rich has a job, which uses his writing ability
Describing hotels on the web with talent and agility

Jim still rides his bike for mile after mile
And delivers Meals and Wheels, which makes the elderly smile

As for me, Trish, I'm still teaching my water aerobics classes
I'm playing senior volleyball, working on my bumps, sets, and passes

There was one sad note to this year gone by
We lost our little dachshund, Rookie, and it made us cry

She was a very loving pet and good to the end
We will definitely miss our fat little friend

Thanks for reading what I had to say
I HOPE YOU HAVE A GREAT HOLIDAY!

SCHREIBER CHRISTMAS POEM, 2008

Greetings to each family member and friend
Another good year has come to an end

With this little poem, I'll try to summarize
The things going on in all five of our lives

As James approaches a birthday beginning with a three
He lives in Chicago where he is happy
His activities include working, carpentry, cooking, and biking
His life in the Midwest is definitely to his liking

On November 24th, Meg turned twenty-seven
For her, living in Athens, Georgia, is heaven
She is now part owner of a bicycle store
And she teaches yoga, which strengthens her core

Rich will turn twenty-four in two thousand nine
He is working in Vietnam, and he's having a good time
His company, Language Corps, gave him the tools
To teach English to students in three different schools

Jim, what can I say about him?
After his bicycle accident in April, things looked kind of grim
But most thankfully, he is now strong and sound
In fact, just last month, he golfed his best round

As for me, Trish, after seven years and seven tries,
In the Scarecrow Contest, I finally won first prize!

MERRY CHRISTMAS AND HAPPY NEW YEAR!

SCHREIBER CHRISTMAS POEM

2009

In this great year of two thousand and nine,
We five Schreibers were never all together at the very same time
So the photo on this card is from a few years ago
I believe in full disclosure and thought you should know

Rich has been in Vietnam teaching English for over a year,
But happily for Christmas he will be here!
His life in Ho Chi Minh City is challenging and fun
Playing soccer with the Saigon Raiders keeps him on the run

Meg lives in Athens, Georgia, a place she really likes
She spends her time teaching yoga and working at Ben's Bikes
She too is coming home for Christmas this year!
Having her in Meadow Vista will give us great cheer!

James lives in Chicago, it is his kind of town
He is planning to buy his own place there and really settle down
He has a good job and friends that are neat
When he too comes home for Christmas, our family will be
Complete!

Not much has changed for Jim and me
We love living in our house, and we are very happy
This summer we took a fun trip to Switzerland, Germany, and
France
James made all the plans and gave us the chance!

I hope your Holidays will be filled with peace, love, and fun
Merry Christmas and Happy New Year to EVERYONE!

SCHREIBER CHRISTMAS POEM

2010

It's Christmastime two thousand and ten
Time to write my family poem again!

For James, life is good in the windy city
He is living with Christy, and she is very pretty
He purchased a condo, which was a good buy
He loves Chicago, and that's no lie

Meg and Eddie live together and hang their hats,
In a cute little house, along with their three cats
Athens, Georgia, is for now their home,
But in the future, they might decide to roam

Back from Vietnam, Rich returned in November
His two years living there, are ones he will always remember
He taught English and played soccer in that far-off place
Graduate school in Chicago will be a big change of pace

Jim is enjoying his golf and biking
Living in Meadow Vista is still to his liking

For me, Trish, my sixtieth birthday is now in the past,
Thanks to my family and friends, I really had a blast

To all of you out there receiving this letter,
I hope your year was good and that 2011 will be even better!

SCHREIBER CHRISTMAS POEM

2011

It has been a great year. I'm happy to report.
For Thanksgiving, we all got together at a Georgia resort.

To attend the gathering, James and Rich drove down.
They both live in Chicago, that toddling town.

James is now engaged to Christy. She is a great catch.
We are all so very happy about the match.

We are happy too that Rich is in graduate school.
A master's in education will be a good tool.

Getting back to the party on November twenty-four,
We celebrated Thanksgiving and so much more.

Meg turned thirty on that very day.
It was fun to celebrate together in a special way.

Meg's bike shop in Athens, Georgia, is doing well.
Her boyfriend is named Eddie, and we think he is swell
Jim is golfing great, and his handicap is lower.
He still rides his bike, maybe just a little slower.

Trish hopes that this poem has given you a smile.
Luckily, you won't have to read another one for a while.

MERRY CHRISTMAS AND HAPPPY NEW

SCHREIBER CHRISTMAS POEM

2012

In this years' poem I have a lot to say
Our family has grown in a wonderful way
As you can see by the photo, there are two new faces
There were two beautiful weddings in two different places

James and Christy were married on a sparkling June day
Their wedding was perfect in every way
The bride and her family had planned things just right
The wonderful reception rocked on through the night

Meg and Eddie tied the knot in early November
It was a cool event we will always remember
There was singing, dancing, and yoga poses
The flowers were handmade, daisies and roses

Rich is writing, playing soccer, and student teaching
He is getting close to the goals for which he's been reaching
Candis, his girlfriend, is smart, nice, and pretty
They both live in Chicago and love the city

The Meadow Vista Schreibers are on an even keel
Jim is still golfing, biking, and gardening with zeal
I'm teaching my fitness classes at the Auburn Racquet Club
I feel so fortunate to be able to do something I love

This Christmas, we are traveling to old Santa Fe
It will be fun to celebrate the holiday in a different way
My poem is pretty short, and I'm sure that is pleasing
I hope everyone has a GREAT HOLIDAY SEASON

SCHREIBER CHRISTMAS POEM

2013

Oh, happiness and joy! Give a big cheer!
The time to compose the family Christmas poem is here!
I'll try to convey in a few short lines,
The family news and all the good times.

For James and Christy, life in Chicago is good
They love their condo and their neighborhood
James works from home on his laptop computer
Christy works at Pepper Construction. At her HR job, she is super.

In the past year, Meg and Eddie purchased a home.
They like living in Athens and don't want to roam.
Meg teaches yoga and keeps the books for Ben's Bikes.
Eddie is developing Athens Public TV, which is something he likes.

For Rich in Chicago, it is his first year of teaching.
With enthusiasm and creativity, his students he's reaching.
He is also coaching and playing soccer, his favorite game.
All these things keep him busy, and no day is the same.

For Jim and me, life is on a great path.
Every day, we are thankful for all that we have.
We love you all, our family and friends.
On that happy note, this poem now ends.

Schreiber Christmas

Poem

2014

This sunlit photo taken by Annie Newboe
Shows our family with a couple of new members in tow
I'm very excited to write the poem this day
Because so many happy events have come our way

In June, Christy and James became parents of a baby boy
He is handsome, healthy, and a wonderful joy
Jack is his name, and it fits him to a tee
He is loved and welcomed by our family

Meg and Eddie are also jumping into the parenthood ring
They are expecting a baby sometime next spring
Their two cats will now have to take a backseat
Having another grandchild will be such a treat

Anna is the new face in the photo on the card
When Rich met her, he fell for her hard
They are now engaged and plan to marry next year
She is a wonder girl and adds to our cheer

With all these happy events that have come our way
Grandpa Jim and Grandma Trish have only one thing to say
WE ARE GRATEFUL

MY SCARECROW STORY

My husband, Jim, was the one who originally suggested the idea of entering the scarecrow contest. He showed our son, James, and me an article in the *Auburn Journal* encouraging readers to enter the Auburn Community Festival Scarecrow Contest. The article showed a photo of the previous year's winner: a scarecrow striding along, picking up popcorn with a vacuum cleaner. "How clever," I thought. I had never made a scarecrow before, but I was excited to try.

The first order of business was to come up with an idea. I teach water aerobics classes, so I decided to make a scarecrow that looked like a water aerobics participant. I didn't want my scarecrow to be floppy. I decided to make the body out of chicken wire. Wearing heavy leather gloves, I found I could squeeze and manipulate the wire into arms, legs, a body, and a head. Then I carefully wrapped masking tape over the entire figure. Over the masking tape, I used panty hose to simulate the scarecrow's "skin." I then dressed my creation in one of my old swimsuits, put a pair of webbed water exercise gloves on the hands and my old water shoes on the feet. On the head, I placed a red swimming cap and a pair of sunglasses, then I tossed a beach towel over the figure's shoulders. The effect was really good, I thought.

The morning of the contest, I headed over to the ARD Park where the festival was being held. Excitement was in the air, with all kinds of people, young and old, setting up their scarecrows. I couldn't believe the elaborate displays that were being constructed. I quickly realized my water aerobics scarecrow was out of her league. I wasn't too surprised when I didn't win anything that first year in 2002. I could see I was going to have to do more than just slap a scarecrow together, if I were to win a prize.

116

So the following year, I started planning for the contest way ahead of time. I planted gourds and pumpkins because I had observed that many of the winning entries were adorned with them. And I wracked my brain to think of a clever way to incorporate the word "crow" into the title of my scarecrow. After all, "Vincent Van Crow" had won second place in the last festival. I finally came up with the idea of making "Frosty the Crowman." I was ready to try again.

I spent hours and hours making old Frosty. Again, chicken wire was the main foundation. This time, I made the figure in three sections, just like a real snowman. I won't go into all the details of building my entry, I'll just say, I was very proud of my creation.

Unlike the year before, this year I really thought I had a good chance at placing in the competition. My display looked great. Frosty the Crowman stood tall and straight surrounded by several baskets of pumpkins and gourds. On the grass, I spread white popcorn to look like snow. I had to admit though that there were a lot of other excellent scarecrows. At 3:00 p.m. when the awards were announced, I sat nervously on a straw bale waiting to hear the results. Fifth place was announced, then fourth, oh please, please let me be third. I knew I probably wasn't good enough for first or second, but I thought maybe third. Well, it was not to be. I was out of the money.

My first reaction was, I'm never entering this contest again, but after a few days, I started thinking of what I could do for the next year. In 2004, I finally won third place with my entry entitled "King Midas." Encouraged by my third place win, I was hooked on participating in the yearly scarecrow contest. I told myself that now that I had won a third place, I would just be entering the contest for the creative experience. I wouldn't care if I won or lost. After all, hadn't I always told my kids, "It doesn't matter if you win or lose, as long as you are having fun." But after "Crow Magnon Man" and "Crowbot" finished out of the money, I realized I *did* care about winning. I cared a lot. It bugged me that one guy, Kurt Barton, won first prize every year. I began to think of him as my "archenemy," even though he was a friendly, soft-spoken man, not to mention a first class artist.

In my frustration, I wrote the following letter to the editor of the *Auburn Journal.*

Dear Editor,

I was very happy after reading "Word on the Street" in Oct. 23's Journal. The quote from six-year-old, Kendall Maynard, saying that his favorite scarecrow was "Crowbot" made my day.

I have been participating in the scarecrow contest at the Auburn Community Festival for five years. To say that the competition is stiff is definitely an understatement. This year, although the prize money was astronomical, it seemed like there were fewer entries.

I think this is because people feel like they can't compete against a few entrants that win year after year. Most of us don't have the vehicles or resources to create entries on such a large scale. It definitely appears that the contest has changed from scarecrow to scarecrows.

I'm not sure what the remedy is for this. I enjoy the large, elaborate entries as much as anyone. Maybe a new elite category should be created for these super achievers. I do think that there are a lot of us out there who still want to try to create a single scarecrow that kids like Kendall Maynard will enjoy.

Trish Schreiber, Meadow Vista

Sending the letter probably wasn't the best thought-out move, but it was an honest statement of the way I felt. My kids and Jim kidded me about the letter. I guess I could see the humor.

By now, participating in the scarecrow contest was becoming "my thing." My water aerobics students asked me, "Are you making a scarecrow this year?" My family and friends also wanted to know if I plan to continue entering the contest. Their interest and support made me want to keep competing in the contest.

After losing again in 2006 with my "Happy Halloweenie" entry, I was still searching for the perfect idea. I wanted to create a scarecrow that would incorporate humor and be related to the fall season. That year, 2007, our yard was covered with fallen acorns. I had always loved the shape and feel of acorns. I started collecting buckets full of the brown torpedo-shaped nuts. Then I had my brainstorm—"Mr. Acorn." I would build a scarecrow spoofing Mr. Peanut, the iconic Planters Peanuts mascot and logo.

Once I had my idea, the fun part began. I had to work out how I would make the figure. I wanted the body to be the shape of an acorn and also be covered with acorns. For me, the most enjoyable part of creating my scarecrows has always been the problem-solving aspect of the endeavor. I have to figure out what materials to use and what I can realistically achieve with my limited building skills. One thing I've never shied away from is spending money on my entries. In fact, buying all the spray paint, tape, glue, and chicken wire is one the things I enjoy doing the most. Of course, I also try to recycle stuff and use some of the old wood we have stored out in the barn.

The biggest challenge I faced in creating Mr. Acorn was how to get the figure to stand up securely on one straight leg with the other leg bent— Mr. Peanut's recognizable stance. I realized I would need a strong stake leg that would hold him up. I then came up with the idea of having a stand that the stake could be fitted into. Making a sturdy wooden stand was outside of my ability. I asked Jim if he could make it for me. After some grumbling, he took on the project. The wooden stand made all the difference and solved the problem of how to get the large figure to stand erect. The acorn body was made out of chicken wire covered with brown duct tape. I then had to find a way to attach all the acorns I had collected to the body. I drove down to my favorite store, Michaels. There, I pondered the many different kinds of glues and adhesives. I finally decided to buy several tubes of Amazing GOOP, which turned out to be a good choice. The glue wasn't that sticky when applied, but after twenty-four hours, it set up like cement. I painstakingly applied acorns to the body in sections, allowing each section to dry completely.

There were many more steps to completing my Mr. Acorn scarecrow, like making the top hat and monocle and finding a cane. I also made a big sign saying "Mr. Acorn" and another sign with a painting of Mr. Peanut, Mr. Acorn's famous cousin.

On the day of the contest, we got to the park early to set up. Jim, as he did every year, helped me carry everything to my spot and helped me erect my display. Without Jim's help, I wouldn't be able to compete. After Mr. Acorn was in place, I immediately began to get good feedback from the people walking past my entry. Maybe this year would be *my* year.

In the afternoon, my sister-in-law, Betty, my niece, Sondra, and her little kids arrived at the park. They were my faithful cheering crowd, and they came every year to support me. At three o'clock, I was again sitting on a straw bale awaiting my fate. Fifth place, fourth place, third place, and second place were announced. Then I heard my name called. Mr. Acorn had won first place! I ran up to the stage to receive my ribbon and envelope, containing $1,000. I shook hands with Derrick Rothe, the founder of the Auburn Community Harvest Festival. I thanked him, and I also thanked Jim for all his help. I had finally won the scarecrow contest. I was glad, but I wasn't used to winning, and it felt weird.

The first chance I got, I called our son, James, on my cell phone. You see, he had also made a scarecrow that first year that I entered the contest. His Vincent Van Crow entry won second place. I had always been envious of his right-off-the-bat success. He was very happy for me. Talking to him made me feel so good.

Now in 2014, I'm working on my thirteenth scarecrow entry. It will be titled, "My Scarecrow Story." I've done paintings of my past twelve scarecrow entries, which I will display on cardboard panels. I plan to construct a seated scarecrow figure that looks just like me. The Trish figure will be sitting on a bench holding a book titled *My Scarecrow Story*. There will be room on the bench for little kids to sit and have their photo taken alongside the reading scarecrow. I have high hopes for this years' entry, but then I always have great expectations. I guess I'll just have to wait and see how this chapter of my scarecrow story turns out.

BAD TRIP

"I just don't want to gain any weight on this vacation," Rich told me as we sat in the car in the parking lot at a small shopping center. I had taken the rental car and driven to the super market in a desperate attempt to find something he would eat. The problem that had been brewing all summer had come to a head on this family trip to Myrtle Beach.

I remembered the first time Rich had left a salami sandwich uneaten on the paper plate I had brought him while he was watching TV. I thought maybe that was the start of the whole terrible thing. Now just a few months later, it was incredible to realize how the whole family had adjusted to the eating restrictions Rich placed on himself. All the foods he ate had to be low-fat, and he wouldn't even consider eating any kind of candy or dessert. At home, Rich's new way of eating hadn't seemed that bad, but during this family reunion in South Carolina, it was becoming obvious that there was something really wrong.

It seemed as though everything on the trip revolved around food, which was normal when the Schreiber family got together. There were four families staying in three different condos, a couple of blocks from the beach. Meals had been difficult. The big group made eating out hard. Often, the group would order pizza or go out for fast-food. These were things Rich wouldn't eat. So I had brought him to this Kroger Market. "How about this frozen spinach?" I handed the box to Rich so he could check the number of calories listed on the back.

"I guess it's OK," Rich mumbled.

We continued down the freezer aisle and added a package of veggie chicken nuggets to the cart. I knew my handsome twelve-year old son was starving himself. I'd seen enough Oprahs to know that Rich was suffering from anorexia nervosa. While watching shows about the disease, I'd always viewed the families of these emaciated teenage girls with contempt. "How could any parent let that happen to their child?" I had wondered. Well, now I knew; it wasn't that simple. With all my own insecurities, the one thing I'd always believed about myself was that I was a good mother. But would a "good mother" have a son with a psychological disease?

The next day, all the men went golfing and the women set out to beach with the kids. The older cousins helped herd the younger ones along. Once there, we spread out our towels. I watched as the kids stripped off their tee shirts and cover-ups and ran down to the water. My older nieces wore bikinis and had fantastic figures. They drew a lot of stares from the guys on the beach. The three Nelli kids, who were roughly the same ages as our children, were just average kids, not fat and not skinny. Betty, Jeanne, and I watched the cousins. Rich sat by himself on a towel, his knees drawn up to his chest.

"Hey, Rich you should go in the water," Aunt Betty said. "Come on take off your sweatshirt, it's roasting out here."

And she was right, of course. It was hot, but Rich looked like he was freezing. Betty just wouldn't let up, and finally, Rich got up and pulled off his shirt. And there he was for everyone in the family to see, my anorexic son with his razor sharp shoulder blades and sunken stomach.

I always look back on that trip as one of the low points of my life. We've never talked that much about it. Rich slowly got better, and now, he is a strong, handsome adult. I can almost forget the thing ever happened, but there are some photos from that terrible time. One photo in particular breaks my heart. Rich and I are standing side by side: a frightened mother and her starving son.

HAPPINESS CLASS

I came to the pursuit of happiness class, not knowing what to expect. In the Placer School for Adults catalog the class description read, "What makes you happy? What interferes with that happiness? How can you become more fulfilled? Those were the very questions I am always thinking and thinking about, so I decided to sign up for the class.

I used to love the musical group Poco when I was in college. In one of their songs, there was a verse, "Who has the right to happiness?" That line spoke to me because I've never really felt that I deserved to be happy. I don't think I've earned the right. Even though Thomas Jefferson stated in the Declaration of Independence:

We hold these truths to be self-evident, that all men are created equal, that they are endowed by their Creator with certain unalienable Rights, that among these are Life, Liberty and the pursuit of happiness.

Maybe the class would help me figure out why I struggle with being happy.

The first Tuesday night of the class, the room was unbearably hot. All the participants sat around the Formica tables that had been pushed together to form a big conference-like table. We all eyed each other. Stuart, the instructor, handed out a typed agenda. I liked that. It showed organization. We followed the agenda. The participants all gave a brief summaries of their lives and stated what they wanted to get out of the class. Then Stuart talked about his joys, which he classified as ten pursuits. He also discussed the challenges in his life. He said he would like each of us to give a similar presentation sometime during the course of the eight-week class. People started to volunteer for different dates. I didn't raise my hand not because I'm shy about talking in front of a group, but because I just wasn't sure yet what the experience would be all about.

As it has turned out, I've learned something from each person that has talked. I've been surprised by everyone's openness and honesty. Tom started everything off with a very impressive presentation. He shared the music that he likes and some books that have helped him. Tom made the point that there is duality in life. You can't have the good without the bad. Many of his joys were also his challenges. Tom got the whole process off to a good start.

As the classes went by, there were certain parts of the participants' presentations that really stuck with me. When Colleen brought out her hand puppet and I saw how people reacted, I realized that art really has a positive effect. When Pam described seeing all the used tissues in the counselor's wastebasket and how she decided to dry her tears and carry on, that story affected me. When Mary said she put on a happy face at the job she didn't like, that resonated with me. I felt like half the time, I've been slapping on that fake happy face myself. When Sandy shared her stacks of books, I thought, "Wow, here is someone who is really trying to figure these things out." When Tim gave his sincere explanation of the cyclical perspective, again I was impressed with how much research and thought he had put into his personal pursuit of happiness. When second Sandy talked about the stories she tells herself, that statement struck a chord with me too. When Jean and Gelene spoke, I admired both of them for the good lives they have led.

The person that made the biggest impression on me was Pam because she *is* a happy person. The buoyancy she talked about shines through. It was great to hear her talk about her work. I would love to have her as a boss. Just the fact that someone has achieved happiness gives me hope.

So now it is time for me to give my presentation. I think Stuart's format of stating my joys and then outlining my challenges is a good one. Like Tom, many of my joys are also my challenges, but I'll start with my joys.

The number one joy on my list is my three children. The happiest time of my life was when they were growing up and living at home. I loved being a mom. I loved volunteering in their classrooms, driving them to practices, helping with their homework, and making their meals. I always tried to be a nice mom. I wasn't big on discipline, and really, my husband, Jim, wasn't either. But our kids, for the most part, were always really good. They all had great grades in school, and we were proud of them.

My career as a group fitness instructor is another one of my joys. I got into teaching classes just after I turned forty. When my kids were little, I went to an exercise class at Placer Hills School called jog jazz. I loved the instructor, and when she started teaching at the Auburn Racquet Club, I followed her there. After years of attending classes, I wanted to try to teach. I took a course in Sacramento at a place called the FIRM. After that, I studied hard and took the IDEA certification exam, and luckily, I passed. Once I was certified, I could teach at the Racquet Club. The first class I was given was a water aerobics class. I didn't have any experience with water aerobics, but I had to get my foot into the door at the club. As it turned out, getting into water aerobics is the best thing that could have happened for me. I love the older participants, and it is a gentler form of exercise that I hope to be able to teach for several more years. I also teach two low-impact aerobics classes, which I really enjoy. My classes give structure to my week. I like the creativity of picking out the music and choreographing my routines. I've been teaching for twenty-two years now, and I'm proud of that.

Art is also one of my joys. Like Stuart, I get a real lift out of looking at art. I also make art or, as I call it, my little projects. I'm always making cards and decorations. For the last thirteen years, I've entered a scarecrow in the Auburn Community Festival's scarecrow contest. I guess it has become sort of my thing. I've won a few prizes over the years, and one year, I even won first place. I continue to enter the contest though, not for the prizes, but because I truly enjoy thinking up an idea and then figuring out how to construct it. I consider my scarecrows a form of art.

Another thing that gives me joy is Christmas. I'm not at all religious, so my love of the holiday is on a more shallow and even a commercial level. I like the days leading up to Christmas better than the actual day.

The tasks that many people hate are things I like to do. For example, I enjoy sending out Christmas cards. We always have a photo card of our family, and for the last several years, I've written a poem to accompany the card. Addressing the cards is fun for me too. I watch some old Christmas movie, while I stuff the envelopes and put on the stamps and address labels. But my favorite part of Christmas is decorating. I have a lot of beautiful Christmas decorations that I've collected over the years. I put them up in the same spots in the living room each year, and they make me happy. I also love decorating the tree. Jim and I finally realized an artificial tree made more sense for us. I hated to give up the live-tree tradition, but I do like the fake tree we have, and once I put all our beautiful ornaments on, it looks very good. Over the years, I've expanded our outdoor light display to its current glory. I can honestly say that lights make me happy. I enjoy the task of putting them up and taking them down. What I enjoy most though is just looking at them.

Another thing that gives me joy is walking with my girlfriends. There are five of us, and we walk on Sunday mornings. In 2002, we participated in the Avon Three-Day Breast Cancer Walk. This sixty-mile walk from San Jose to San Francisco was quite an experience and helped to bond us together. We all use the walks as impromptu therapy sessions. We talk over our problems, and it is great to have that outlet and support. I feel very lucky to have these four dear friends.

Books make me happy. I enjoy reading and listening to them. I mainly like fiction, but I also enjoy autobiographies, biographies, and memoirs. I never listen to the radio in my car. I only listen to books on CD. I get coffee at Starbucks and then sit in the parking lot and drink the coffee and listen to a book. I never mind the fifteen-minute drive from Meadow Vista to Auburn, because I'm listening to a book. I also listen to books on a little CD player as I walk up and down our driveway for exercise. I read books in bed every night before I go sleep. In fact, it is difficult for me to fall asleep unless I read.

Our house and our yard give me a lot of pleasure. We have lived at 1480 Combie Road in Meadow Vista since 1978. When you live in a house for that long, it becomes very comforting and dear to you—a home and a haven. I love our acreage with all the oaks, cedars, and ponderosa pines.

I'm not that fond of housework, but I do love working out in the yard. Mowing, raking, and gardening are tasks that I enjoy.

These next joys might also be called my guilty pleasures. They are food, coffee, alcohol, and television. I definitely get enjoyment from these things. I love food. Coffee gives me a lift. Alcohol gives me a brief euphoric feeling. Television has been my friend since childhood. I have spent countless happy hours watching my favorite shows.

Finally, my marriage gives me joy and contentment. As it says in the Johnny Cash song, "We got married in a fever, hotter than a pepper sprout." That early passion got us together, but we've had to work hard and compromise to keep the relationship going. Jim and I will celebrate our thirty-eighth wedding anniversary on November 13. I've spent more time with Jim than any other person in my life. Now that he is retired and our kids are out of the house, we are spending even more time together. I'm glad I'm not alone. I have the security of a long marriage, and most of the time that makes me happy.

So now, I'll try to explain my challenges. This is not as easy as stating my joys. As I said before, many of my joys are also my challenges.

So I'm just going to quickly go down the line.

- I love teaching water aerobics and low-impact aerobics, but I often worry that I'm just going through the motions. After teaching for so many years, I worry that I'm in a rut. I question the quality of my classes.
- My love of Christmas is a real thing. But when the season is over, I always feel a letdown. I know this happens every year, and I try to take positive steps to deal with it. I'm not always successful though. So the peak of the Christmas season is followed by the valley of the gray months of January and February.
- Listening to books is also a challenge in a way. I sometimes think I listen to so many books, because I want to be distracted from the negative thoughts in my head. I have to be careful not to listen to sad books because I've learned they can bring me down. I've been so impressed by all the self-help books that people in the

class have read. For some reason, I just can't seem to get into that kind of reading. I realize this sounds self-defeating.

- Food, I spend so much time purchasing it, preparing it, and eating it. Like so many people, I eat to feel better. I think my appetite for food will always be something that gives me pleasure, but also worry and guilt.

- Alcohol. I have always been very wary of its power. Alcoholism runs all through my family. Having an alcoholic sister and brother has shaped my life. My other two sisters don't drink at all, but I do. I know drinking can makes me happy for short bursts of time. I don't have a problem with drinking, but I still manage to worry about it.

- Coffee, I'm definitely hooked. I have figured out that too much coffee is bad for me. If I have more than sixteen ounces of coffee a day, my mind just starts spinning around with obsessive thoughts.

- Television, I just watch way too much. I could accomplish so much more if I wasn't sitting on the sofa staring at our beautiful flat-screen TV.

- My marriage. I don't think Jim and I inspire each other to be the best version of ourselves. Jim is very passive, and I get so frustrated with him at times. He is basically a more contented person than I am, and he doesn't seem to struggle with the same demons that I have. I wish he was more serious and I know he would like me to be more easygoing.

- Finally, my biggest challenge is having periods of sadness. I have down periods when I don't have energy and I feel bad. Sometimes these depressed times are triggered by a sad event. But I think most of the time, I just create the negative mood in my head.

I know I am into self-criticism, and I can get into a circular pattern of thinking I'm not accomplishing anything and yet I don't take the steps to rectify the situation by doing positive things. So my biggest challenge is myself. I actually don't even like trying to write about this because it just seems like complaining.

When I was little, my mom often repeated Abraham Lincoln's famous quote, "Folks are usually about as happy as they make up their minds to be." This would make me so mad. It didn't seem to be true for me because, even as a child, I had times of feeling sad for no apparent reason. I wanted to be happy, but I just couldn't feel happy. I had many worries. I worried about getting polio and the world being blown up by an atom bomb. I worried about all the poor animals and people in the world.

Now that I'm an adult, I've been able to come to better terms with my tendency toward melancholy. This class has given me some more tools to work with. I looked up "Happiness Quotes" on the computer, and the one that really spoke to me was from John Barrymore: "Happiness often sneaks in through a door you didn't know you left open."

I do get those unexpected feelings of happiness, and when I do, *I am grateful*.

READING WITH EDITH

As usual, I was feeling guilty. Why wasn't I doing any volunteer work? After all, I had plenty of free time. Shouldn't I be helping out in the community somehow? It was easy when the kids were in school. I had many opportunities to volunteer. I loved being an art docent in all three kids' classrooms in elementary school. I manned the student store in the middle school cafeteria. It was fun being a team mom for soccer. I even coached my daughter's basketball team, which was very rewarding. When the kids got to high school, I worked with the Parent Club and was copresident for several years. I liked that job. It wasn't hard and it sounded important. That was the thing about me, I wanted to do a volunteer job, but it couldn't be too difficult or depressing.

So when I saw the poster in the library, seeking volunteers to teach people to read, I thought, "That doesn't sound too hard, maybe I could do that." I called the number on the poster and found out there was a mandatory training session in a few weeks. Perfect, I would attend.

The training was held at the Placer County Library in Auburn in the Beecher Room. The class started at 9:00 a.m., and Starbucks coffee was provided, which was nice. The woman leading the class showed us how to fold a piece of paper in three sections to make a little nameplate to place in front of us on the table. We then proceeded to go around the group and tell a little bit about ourselves. There were about fifteen women in attendance, and most of them were teachers or retired teachers. I began to think I really wasn't nearly as qualified as most of the people in the training class.

The woman heading up the program explained that the people we would be teaching were called "learners" and that we would be called "tutors." She discussed the resources of the library that would be available to us as tutors. The class lasted about three hours, and at the end, everyone was asked to fill out several pages of paperwork. When I turned in my application, I sort of doubted that I would ever be called.

So I was surprised when a few days later, a woman from the literacy program called and said they had a possible "learner" for me. Her name was Edith Miller, and she lived right in Meadow Vista where I lived. The woman explained that Edith had suffered a stroke and had some difficulty speaking. She had been working with a woman named Carol. Edith felt that reading out loud with Carol was really helping her speech. Unfortunately, Carol had moved away, so Edith was looking for someone else to read with. I really didn't know what to think. I had imagined I would be teaching some poor janitor or a misunderstood teenager how to read. I wasn't sure how I felt about reading with someone who already knew how to read perfectly well. But in a way, I figured it was good, since I honestly didn't know if I would be able to teach someone to read.

I took the assignment and called Edith on the phone to set up our first meeting. Her voice was deep, and she spoke haltingly. The effects of her stroke were apparent. I'm really not that good at talking on the phone under the best of circumstances. This conversation was especially stilted, with me inadvertently interrupting her before she had finished making a point. We eventually worked things out though, and I agreed to go to her house on the following Tuesday at two o'clock.

At the training class, we had been told that there were literacy materials available for the "tutors" at the library. So I went to the library and asked one of the librarians where I could find the literacy books. She led me to door in the back of the building, which opened to a staircase. I never even knew there was a second floor at the Auburn Library. Anyway, I climbed the stairs to the second-floor offices. I was directed to a bookcase loaded with workbooks. I picked out four books: two copies each of the *Challenger* adult reading series, numbers 7 and 8. These books consisted of short stories, articles, and some poems. There were questions and exercises at the end of each chapter.

The next Tuesday, equipped with the workbooks, I drove to Edith's house. She only lived about a mile and a half away from our house. I was anxious as I pulled into her circular driveway. I really didn't know what to expect from this endeavor. When Edith answered the door, I liked her looks immediately. She was an attractive woman. Her gray hair was cut short, and she wore jeans and an embroidered sweatshirt. I can't remember too much about that first session. I think we read a story that had a tiger in it. We first tried reading in unison. That wasn't working, so we decided to alternate reading paragraphs. Edith read slowly, and some words were difficult for her. She was embarrassed when she couldn't tackle a word, but she was able to deflect the situation with a laugh or shake of her head.

We stuck with the reading workbooks for a while, but eventually, we had read most of the stories and articles. I decided to go to the library to find some new reading material. I found two copies of a little book called *The Acorn People*. It was a simple story about a young man who took a job as a counselor at a camp for physically challenged kids. This book held our interest and was fun to read with lots of good dialogue. Our next book was *Tuesdays with Morrie*. In the book, Mitch Albom visited every Tuesday his old professor and mentor, Morrie Schwartz, who was afflicted with ALS. Edith and I joked that we were also meeting on Tuesdays— Tuesdays with Edith.

It is hard to explain exactly how our friendship developed over the next weeks, months, and years. Our reading sessions were always at Edith's neat and tidy house. We sat at her round wooden dining table to read. Before cracking open our books, we would visit for a few minutes. Edith had many challenges in her life, but she never let them get her down for long. She had a strong Christian faith and lived her beliefs. Like me, she had three kids. Her oldest child was my age. Her husband, Louie, was usually at home when we were reading. He would give me a short, friendly greeting and then shuffle off to another part of the house, so we could get down to reading. The age gap between us never seemed to matter. Edith was fun to be with and had a good sense of humor.

The majority of our time though was always spent reading. I figured out that if a book was too long, it really didn't work for us. Also, I didn't want to read anything about violence or sex with Edith. So I started looking in the young adult section of the library for our reading material. As I've mentioned before, it was necessary to have two copies of any book we read, so we could each hold our own book. As it turned out, many of the books were Newberry Award winners. I guess the library was more likely to have multiple copies of these award-winning books.

Edith and I didn't think about keeping track of the books we'd read until a few years into our relationship. We did eventually start keeping track of the books in Edith's spiral notebook. We also tried to remember all the past books that we had read together. Here is a partial list of the titles:

Patty Reed's Doll; Hatchet; Call to Courage; Sara, Plain and Tall; Shiloh; Strider; Dear Mr. Henshaw; Olive's Ocean; Boy of the Painted Cave; The Island of the Blue Dolphins; Justin Morgan Had a Horse; Boy; Sounder, Beezus and Ramona; Bridge to Terabithia; Frozen Fire; Misty of Chincoteague; Red Bird; The Sign of the Beaver; Tuck Everlasting; The Best Christmas Pageant Ever; and *Out of the Dust* (we actually read this one twice). All these books were wonderful, and I really enjoyed reading them out loud with Edith.

Edith's speech has definitely improved in the years that we have been reading together. After she has read a long paragraph especially clearly, I'd say, "That was good reading." I love to hear her voice, and I think she likes my voice too. Edith has always been very appreciative of me coming over to read with her. She thanks me after every session and has given me many generous gifts. I really feel I should be thanking *her*. Our relationship makes me feel good. I'm so glad I met Edith. She is someone I love and admire. I hope I will have many more "Tuesdays with Edith."

My Cousin George

Sitting at my home computer, I clicked the "flight status" prompt.

"Oh no!" I gasped.

"Oh no what?" my husband, Jim, called down from upstairs.

"Our flight from Sacramento to Denver is delayed. We're not going to make our connection to Lincoln," I moaned.

All along I had been worried about this possibility, and now it had happened—the worst-case scenario. It wouldn't have been that big of a deal, except that I was scheduled to meet my long lost cousin George at the Lincoln Airport. George and I had been in e-mail contact for a couple of years ever since the Cather Foundation had uncovered his whereabouts. He was my mother's sister's only child. We shared the same claim to fame: Willa Cather was our great aunt.

You don't know who Willa Cather is? Don't feel badly. A lot of people these days aren't familiar with the name. Anyway, she was an acclaimed American author. Every year, her life and legacy are celebrated at the annual Willa Cather Spring Conference in Red Cloud, Nebraska. You see, Red Cloud was where Willa grew up. The little town is depicted in many of her novels under several different names. Many years ago, one woman, Mildred Bennett, started a campaign to save as many buildings as possible that were connected to Willa Cather and her writings. Bennett and her group of locals, the Willa Cather Pioneer Memorial (now the Cather Foundation), were very successful in their endeavors. Today, you can visit Cather's childhood home, the Opera House where her high school graduation was held, and several other buildings. All these structures have been preserved. In fact, the Cather Foundation frequently boasts that "the largest living memorial to an author in the country is located in Red Cloud, Nebraska."

So anyway, getting back to George, my cousin. I hadn't seen him since we were kids. He lived in Pennsylvania and only came to Denver a couple of times with his parents. At that time, I thought he was kind of strange. He had blond hair and looked a little bit like the actor, Jay North, who played Dennis the Menace on the TV show. My main memory of him was playing together by the lily pond at our house on Cedar Avenue.

Why we were out of touch for all these years is sort of hard to say. I always had the impression that he didn't care to be in contact with anyone. I know my parents kept up with him, but after they died, the communication stopped.

My thing is corresponding with the family. I send out Christmas cards every year and try to "keep up" with siblings, nieces, nephews and cousins. I love e-mails and Facebook. They are great for helping me to stay connected to the family, even if it is on a superficial level. I was glad to get George's e-mail address and start corresponding with him. Here is a portion of my first e-mail to him:

> Dear George,
>
> I was very happy when I heard from Jim Southwick that he had located you. I'm really sorry that I have been out of touch for all these years. I definitely remember playing with you when you visited Denver. I was a shy little girl, and I was always nervous about being introduced to new kids, but I recall that we got along well. I think we were even pen pals for a while.

In turn, George e-mailed back:

> Dear Trish,

It was great to hear from you. I certainly remember the visits to Denver. I am actually surprised to hear that you were shy as a child. I was probably so shy myself that I wouldn't have noticed. I still am on the shy side. If I remember correctly, you and Margaret were very interested in horses back then. I remember going riding once at a bridle path in or near Denver.

I was quite surprised hearing from Jim Southwick. It was actually the first time I had heard anything from the Cather side of the family since Mother's funeral in 1984. I do hope we can keep in touch. I guess I assumed the Cather side of the family had just sort of forgotten about me, and it is nice to know that this is not true.

So our e-mail correspondence began. I liked the way George wrote, although he never shared much about his personal life or current circumstances. About all I really knew about him was that he lived in an apartment in Manhattan. In 2009, I broached the idea of having him attend the Cather Spring Conference. I didn't follow through with the idea though, mainly because I was nervous about spending three days with someone I really didn't know. In 2010 though, I proposed the idea again, and this time, George seemed interested in coming to Nebraska. I e-mailed him:

Dear George,

I just checked the Cather Foundation website, and the information about the Spring Conference is now available. You can register online or by mail. I am planning on attending the conference on Friday and Saturday (June 4th & 5th). It will be no problem for my husband and me to pick you up on Thursday, June 3rd in Lincoln. It is a nice three-hour drive down to Red Cloud. I think you will like my husband, Jim. He is a friendly, low-key person, and he gets along well with John and

Margaret (our cousins). Anyway, I'm looking forward to the conference and getting to know you.

George explained that he rarely travelled and hadn't been out of New York in nine years. At first, he planned to take the train to Lincoln, because he wasn't crazy about flying, but in the end he wrote this:

Dear Trish,

I have finally made the flight reservations. I am arriving in Lincoln on Delta/Skywest flight # 4590 at 3:35 PM on Thursday, June 3, 2010. I will be leaving Lincoln on Delta/Skywest flight # 4548 at 4:25 PM on Sunday, June 6, 2010. I should definitely be there before you arrive on the third.

Thanks for your cell number. Unfortunately, I do not have one myself. I have been thinking of getting some sort of inexpensive one for the trip, but have not done so yet.

I wrote back:

Dear George,

It will be great to meet you next week. We will probably plan to have dinner in Lincoln, if that is OK with you. After that, we will drive to Red Cloud. In the past, we've stopped at the Walmart in Hasting to buy snacks. As I've mentioned before, my only worry is missing our connection in Denver. This probably won't happen, but if it does, I'm not sure how we will be able to figure out what to do. Perhaps it would be worthwhile for you to purchase a short-term cell phone for the trip, as you proposed, just in case.

You are all set at the Green Acres Motel, so no worries there. See you soon!

Love, Trish

From all indications this trip was going to be way out of George's comfort zone, a big, scary step for him. So when I realized we weren't going to make it to Lincoln at the scheduled time, I really felt terrible. I was sick about it. After an almost comical call to United reservations, I learned the earliest we could get to the Lincoln Airport would be 11:45 p.m., almost seven hours later than our planned time to meet George.

Of course, I called George right away. Luckily, he had purchased a cell phone for the trip. If he hadn't, I don't know what I would have done. He was probably already on his plane, so I left a very apologetic message. When we got to the Sacramento Airport, I called him again and spoke with him for the first time. I liked his voice. He was understanding and said he "knew it wasn't my fault." But I could hear a little bit of desperation in his voice. I felt terrible. I was responsible for this situation. Didn't I know all along that the layover time between the flights was too short? I suggested to George that maybe he could take a cab into Lincoln and do a little sightseeing to kill time. This idea seemed to overwhelm him. "No," he replied, "I better just wait here at the airport."

When I got off the phone, I turned to my husband, "Oh, Jim, this is awful. George seems pretty anxious, and it's all my fault." In marriages, there are times when your spouse can really support you, or they can point out your mistakes and make you feel worse. Luckily, this was a time when I was given sympathetic support.

"Trish, I know you feel badly, but George will be all right. It's just one of those things. There's not much we can do about it."

Oh, how I appreciated this. I wasn't alone. Jim had my back.

As it turned out, the plane leaving Sacramento was very delayed due to "mechanical problems." As we sat in the waiting area, we witnessed several agitated travelers who were realizing they weren't going to make their connections. Several times, it was announced that boarding would begin in twenty minutes, and then the time would come and go.

While we waited, I had an idea. I had the phone number for the Cather Foundation in Red Cloud, so I gave them a call. I explained the situation, that my cousin, George, was stranded at the Lincoln Airport. I asked if they knew of anyone arriving in Lincoln that could bring George down to Red Cloud. Well, after several phone calls back and forth, it was arranged that George would be able to get a ride. Again, I was so glad that George had purchased a cell phone; our cell phones made the whole arrangement possible.

We finally boarded the plane and had an uneventful flight to Denver. We still had a couple of hours to kill at the Denver airport until our next plane left for Lincoln. I called George again and was so relieved to hear that he had just arrived at the Green Acres Motel in Red Cloud. I was very happy that the arrangements to get him to Red Cloud had worked out. We made a plan to meet outside our rooms at the motel the next morning at 8:00 a.m.

Now that I knew George was safely at the motel, I felt an incredible weight of worry was lifted off my shoulders. Jim and I shared a turkey sandwich at a Sara Lee Sandwich Shoppe. At the next table, I observed a family of travelers. The little boy was trying to get the attention of his dad who was grumpily ignoring him. The mom looked frazzled but was trying to engage and entertain the son. From what I was observing, it seemed to me an example of what my girlfriends and I liked to describe as the husband being a "big baby." Again, I was just so grateful that Jim had been helpful and supportive throughout this long travel day. After our sandwich, we both got a cup of yogurt. Now, I was actually enjoying myself.

The small jet to Lincoln left on time. The flight lasted just over an hour. I rested my head on Jim's shoulder and dozed off for a while. As we were landing, I saw several lightning flashes off in the distance, but the plane touched down safely with no turbulence. It was almost midnight by the time we made our way through the sleepy little airport to the rental car counter. Jim signed all the papers and was given the keys to our rental car, a roomy, white Chevy sedan.

The drive down to Red Cloud that night was one I will never forget. We were virtually the only car on the highway, and as we sped through the darkness, the wide Nebraska sky was illuminated with constant flashes of sheet lightning, a beautiful light show.

The featured novel for the conference was Willa Cather's early novel, *O Pioneers*. Both Jim and I had read it in preparation, but I had also purchased an audio version of the book, and we listened to it as we drove. About an hour into the journey, it began to rain hard. It felt like we were hurtling through space in our snug automobile. The actress on the CD was reading Willa Cather's wonderful words: "Carl sat musing until the sun leaped above the prairie, and in the grass about him all the small creatures of day began to tune their tiny instruments. Birds and insects without number began to chirp, to twitter, to snap and whistle, to make all manner of fresh shrill noises. The pasture was flooded with light; every clump of ironweed and snow-on-the-mountain threw a long shadow, and the golden light seemed to be rippling through the curly grass like the tide racing in."

Those insects Cather wrote about, were smashing into the windshield along with the heavy rain drops. I didn't even realize that moths could fly around in the rain, but they were out in abundance. I glanced over at Jim, his profile was illuminated in the glow of the dashboard lights. I felt a wave of gratitude that this big, handsome man was my husband.

Finally, at about two-thirty in the morning, we drove into the parking lot of the Green Acres Motel. I had called earlier in the day, and the owners had agreed to leave room number 15 open for us, so we wouldn't have to wake them in the middle of the night. We quickly undressed and got into bed. I was still nervous about meeting George in the morning, but the thoughts didn't keep me awake, I fell asleep quickly.

The alarm buzzed at seven-thirty. I took a quick shower and got dressed. I took the short walk to the office to check in. The friendly woman behind the counter said, "Your cousin has already been in a couple of times for coffee." I thanked her for our room key and went back to number 15 to wait out the last few minutes before I would meet George.

At exactly eight o'clock, I opened the door and stepped out into the morning sun. A few doors down, a big man opened his door, turned, and approached me. I waved a greeting. George said, "You look like a combination of your mom and our grandmother."

When I heard that I was so happy. We were family. We had a connection. My cousin, George, knew Mom and Grandmother Cather. All the worries and problems had been worth it. George and I hugged. Jim came out; I introduced him, then we were off to the Willa Cather Spring Conference.

WILLA CATHER IS MY GREAT AUNT

Willa Cather is my great aunt, or she would be, if she were still alive. You've never heard of her? Oh, don't feel badly. When I mention her name to people, about three-quarters of them, don't know about her. But trust me, she is famous. Just Google her, you'll see.

What does it mean to be related to an iconic American author? I certainly have no claim to her fame. I never even met Willa Cather. She died before I was born. In fact, up until a few years ago, I had read only three of her books: *O Pioneers, Song of the Lark,* and *My Antonia.* My knowledge of Willa Cather was very limited. All that changed when my brother, Rich, died in 2004.

After his death, my sister Katie enlisted me in the task of helping her to decide what to do with a large collection of Willa Cather's letters. How the letters came into Katie's possession is a long story. To tell the tale, would take pages and pages of family background, and the explanation would unearth a spider's nest of family secrets. And though I don't doubt it would make very interesting reading, some things are better left unwritten.

It was an incredible responsibility to decide what to do with the letters. Most of the letters were from Willa Cather to her beloved brother, Roscoe. He was my grandfather, and no, I never met him either. The big deal about the collection was that no one in the literary world knew they existed. We were sitting on a gold mine and that statement is no exaggeration. It would probably make my story more interesting if I could just give you a dollar figure for what the letters were worth, but the terms of the donation forbid that. So I'll just state that the value would be one of the largest monetary amounts you have ever seen on *Antiques Roadshow.*

My part in deciding the fate of the Cather letters turned out to be a fascinating and hellish experience. The fascinating part was my foray into the "Cather World." In April of 2005, I attended my first Willa Cather Spring Conference in Red Cloud, Nebraska. This just happened to be the fiftieth anniversary of the founding of the Willa Cather Pioneer Memorial Educational Foundation. To quote the *Willa Cather Newsletter & Review,* "Mrs. Bennett and seven other founding members of the Board of Governors defined the Foundation's mission, which has evolved into these 'Aims of the WCPM':

"To promote and assist in the development and preservation of the art, literary, and historical collection in relation to the life, time and work of Willa Cather, in association with the Nebraska State Historical Society

"To cooperate with the Nebraska State Historical Society in continuing to identify, restore to their original condition, and preserve places made famous by the writing of Willa Cather

"To provide for Willa Cather a living memorial, through the Foundation, by encouraging assisting scholarship in the field of the humanities

"To perpetuate an interest throughout the world in the work of Willa Cather."

From what I could tell, the WCPM had met their aims. I was blown away by what I saw in Red Cloud. I guess the most impressive thing was the restored Opera House, which was the central location of the conference. The two-story building boasted of a bookstore, a gallery, modern offices, an elevator, a large auditorium, and beautiful, modern restrooms. "Wow!" I thought, "this restoration must have cost a fortune."

Since that first conference I attended was the fiftieth anniversary of the founding of the WCPM (or as it is now called the Willa Cather Foundation), there were many activities honoring the woman who started the whole thing. That woman was Mildred Bennett. There was the dedication of the Mildred Bennett Wall in the upstairs lobby of the Opera House. Also, a film biography about Mildred Bennett titled *Singing Cather's Song* was shown. I started to think, "Just who is being remembered here, Willa Cather or Mildred Bennett?" But as the conference proceeded, it was clear the Willa Cather was the main attraction.

One of the most interesting activities of the conference weekend was touring the Cather childhood home. The little wood-framed house on Cedar Street has been restored to look just the way it would have when Willa and my grandfather, Roscoe Cather, lived there. It struck me as so profound that this home and all its contents had been preserved. In the last few years, I had taken several memoir-writing classes through the local adult school. The participants in these classes were invariably older women, who somehow wanted to save the memories of their childhoods. Their stories would include detailed descriptions of the houses where they grew up—the cherished kitchen table, the old stove, and the linoleum floors. All these things that were so dear to them but no one else really cared about anymore. Willa Cather, it seems, had the same instinct to leave a description of her childhood home. She describes it detail in her novel, *Song of the Lark*, and in the short story, "Old Mrs. Harris."

When I returned home from Nebraska, I set out to read the two volumes, published by the Library of America, of all of Willa Cather's writing. My brother, Rich, had given me the books as Christmas presents several years ago. I loved almost everything I read. *Flavia and Her Artists* was the only story I really couldn't get into. I tackled James Woodress's excellent biography of Willa Cather and Edith Lewis's personal account of her long-time partner. I also read with interest Mildred Bennett's *The World of Willa Cather*. I was becoming better educated about my great aunt, but I would never achieve a literary scholars' intense interest in the minutia of Cather's life and writing.

After attending that first conference in Red Cloud, my sister, Katie, and I traveled to New Jersey to attend another Cather event: The Cather Colloquium at Drew University. The symposium celebrated the gift of several Cather letters, books, and magazines that were donated to the school by a wealthy couple, Finn and Barbara Caspersen. On the plane,

Katie had given me some copies of "our" Willa Cather letters to read. I read with interest one letter to her brother, Roscoe, about her last novel, *Sapphira and the Slave Girl*. Willa wrote, "Sapphira is pronounced with a short 'i,' as in Madeira, Zamira, etc. It is not the Bible "Sapphira" with long 'i,' but an old English name made from the Bible name with the 'i' made short." Later, when we were listening to a talk at the Drew conference. The speaker pronounced Sapphira with a long "i," Katie and I just looked at each other sharing our own secret knowledge.

Eventually, the decision was made that we would donate the collection of Willa Cather letters to the University of Nebraska. I truly feel this was an excellent choice. The University of Nebraska was where Willa Cather attended college and graduated in 1895. Also, UNL is home of the Cather Project and the Willa Cather Archive. Again, there is quite a story behind the donation. And again, I don't want to go into it. After what was a very difficult period for me, all the disputes were ironed out, and the Willa Cather letters officially became the property of the University of Nebraska. Katie and I had decided the collection should be named in honor of our grandparents: the Roscoe and Meta Cather Collection.

After the donation became official, the University of Nebraska planned an event to celebrate the occasion. The symposium was titled, "Cather's Circles: Correspondence and Connections," which was held on June 4, 2008. Some of the top Cather scholars were scheduled to present talks. Janis P. Stout, who would later go on to co-edit *The Selected Letters of Willa Cather* with Andrew Jewell gave the keynote speech in the morning. Then in the afternoon, Sharon O'Brien spoke. I really wanted my three children to come to the event. They all rose to my request and made the pilgrimage to Lincoln. Also, my husband, Jim, my sister, Katie, and my cousins John Ickis and Margaret Fernbacher attended the event.

In the evening, a program was held in the auditorium of the Love Library. The Chancellor of the University, Harvey Perlman, spoke about the importance of the donation to the university. Then I gave this short talk:

"My name is Trish Schreiber. My mother, Margaret, was one of the twin daughters of Roscoe and Meta Cather. Unfortunately, I never met my grandfather, Roscoe Cather. He died before I was born. However, I feel that I have come to know him by reading the wonderful letters that he wrote to Willa Cather, his famous sister. He was the most loving brother and consistently supported his sister. He seems to have been the family peacemaker, who tried to iron out problems between the seven Cather siblings. This is illustrated well in a letter he wrote to Willa in 1929.

"'My dear, you must not think that your family does not appreciate your success. The trouble is you long ago reached a plane so far above our little world that we have no measure to use. And it is hard for us to express ourselves, anything we say or write seems so futile, downright piffle. I am sure that is the way the rest of them feel and as for myself, you have been the biggest single thing in my life. You have always been a pride and a joy and never a single worry to cloud it. I wish I could make you understand what you have been to me from the time I was a little boy and worshipped you literally.' End of quote.

"I feel that as scholars study and read the letters in this collection, they will come to the same conclusion that I have—that Roscoe Cather was an incredible man. He was loving, loyal, and very ethical. I really wish I could have known him. I was fortunate though to have had my grandmother, Meta Cather, in my life. She lived in Denver and was part of all our Shannon family gatherings and holidays while my brother, Rich, my sisters, Katie, Elizabeth, Margaret, and I were growing up. She was always beautifully dressed in wool suits and hats. She wore her silver hair in two little rolled up buns on the nape of her neck. Grandmother Cather could recite countless poems from memory in English and German. She always recited "'Twas the Night Before Christmas" on every Christmas Eve. And we all delighted in the way she said, "He was dressed all in fuuuuur."

"To me, she was a loving, quiet grandmother, but I never really appreciated the amazing things she had accomplished in her life. To quote my mother's handwritten history of Meta Cather's life: "She entered Nebraska University in the fall, 1899, and went right through the four years, being elected to Phi Beta Kappa in her senior year. This was quite a surprise to her and unusual for a young woman at the time." What an understatement. I am glad that through the Roscoe and Meta Cather

Collection, her legacy will live on. Scholars will learn of the important relationship that she had with her sister-in-law, Willa Cather.

"Also, I would like to say something about my dear little mom, Margaret Cather Shannon. While I was growing up, she never really talked much about her famous Aunt Willie. In fact, it was my father, Richard Shannon, who more encouraged his five children to read Cather's books. He tried to get us to appreciate what a privilege it was to have such a distinguished relative. I'm not sure why Mom didn't talk more about her beloved aunt. I feel it might have been that she wanted to respect Willa Cather's desire for privacy. She certainly never used her relationship with her aunt to promote herself. But Mom did write a beautiful memoir titled, *Willa Cather Remembered*. This account is now part of the Roscoe and Meta Cather Collection.

"It begins, 'I first knew Aunt Willa, or rather she knew me, in 1916. My twin sister, Elizabeth, and I were born in Lander, Wyoming, in August of 1915.' When Aunt Willa heard of the twins, she was really thrilled. Dad and she had been very close as children and maintained that relationship throughout their lives. So in 1916, Aunt Willa made the long trip to Wyoming from New York City to see the new babies. She was most interested in everything about the year-old babies who looked exactly alike. Before Mother would put us to bed, Aunt Willa would more or less conceal herself in the nursery and watch and listen to us as we settled down. She claimed that we had a language of our own, and would talk back and forth to each other before we fell asleep.

"The most fascinating part of Mom's memoir is the description she gives of the two visits she and Elizabeth made to Grand Manan Island in New Brunswick, Canada, in 1936 and 1937. I quote Mom here:

"'The days were similar, except for special outings. The four of us would meet at the Main House for breakfast. Then, the four of us would walk to the cottage, and soon after go on the Cliff Walk. It was a foot trail along the cliffs. Aunt Willa knew every turn and tree-many of the places she and Miss Lewis had named, often using names or phrases from *Alice in Wonderland*. At noon, we would be back at the Main House for lunch. Then Aunt Willa and Miss Lewis retired to their cottage for three or four hours. We would see them again around four o'clock when Elizabeth and I walked to the cottage for tea. Those were about the best times. There would be a fire in the fireplace and we would have tea or sherry and a special bread from St. John. It was a grand time of conversation and reading aloud from their favorite books.'

"This account is especially touching when paired with a letter that Willa wrote to her sister-in-law, Meta, on January 16, 1947. I am taking the liberty of quoting directly from her letter.

"'Well dear Meta, no matter what happens in the future, I will have the memory of those two summers when Elizabeth and Margaret visited me at Grand Manan. Everything was lovely then; they enjoyed and appreciated the spots, which I most loved on that remote little island which I fear I shall never see again. Often in the wakeful hours of the night, I think of Margaret and Elizabeth just as they were then, when we used to have gay little dinners, with champagne, down in our funny little cottage on Sunday nights. Youngsters grow up and become totally absorbed in lives of their own, and the amusements of their childhood mean very little to them. But to older people those memories remain important. In showing Margaret and Elizabeth my favorite spots on lovely island, I re-lived all the excitement of my early explorations on Grand Manan. My nieces have outlived those things, but I will never outlive them because at my time of life, one lives backward rather than forward in personal relations and affections that is especially true.' End of quote.

"I think Willa Cather would be gratified to know that her niece, Margaret, recalled the time they spent together on Grand Manan with the same reverence that she did.

"I feel that every generation wants to somehow convey to the younger generation how it was for them growing up. There is a strong desire to preserve the past and ensure that the people we loved are not forgotten. Of course, there is *no* danger of Willa Cather's life and legacy not being kept alive. But even without the scholars, the universities, the historical societies, and the foundations, Willa Cather would live on. Anytime a reader picks up one of her marvelous books, they will be transported into her world. Through her genius and artistry, she has kept her precious memories alive.

"In closing, I want to thank my husband Jim, and our three children—James, Meg, and Rich—for attending this historic event. It means the world to me to have them here tonight. Thank you all for listening."

As I read the last couple of sentences of my talk, I looked out into the audience where my kids and husband were sitting. My voice cracked with emotion, and tears came to my eyes. I guess this was my moment in the spotlight. All along the journey of deciding what to do with the Willa Cather letters, I had fantasized about somehow parlaying the situation into some kind of fame for myself. And if I were a really good writer and didn't mind ruffling a lot of feathers, maybe I could have written the whole story and had it published in a national magazine. My parents' beloved *New Yorker* would have been the ultimate dream. But it was all just a dream. As I wrote earlier, Willa Cather is my great aunt, or she would be if she were still alive. I certainly have no claim to her fame.

1st Christmas Card

3rd Christmas Card

7th Christmas Card

13th Christmas Card

19th Christmas Card

23rd Christmas Card

35th Christmas Card

Christmas in Meadow Vista

Dad in his gardening clothes with the tennis court in the background

Me and Meg in the hospital right after she was born

Me and the other two Stupid Human participants
on the David Letterman Show

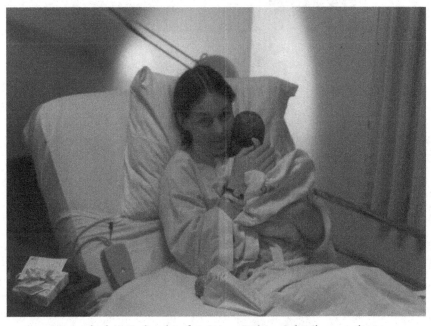

Me in the hospital right after James Robert Schreiber was born

Me, Margaret and Mom

Mom in the formal garden by the weeping mulberry tree

My Century Plant

My childhood home

My first place winner, Mr Acorn

My mother with her famous aunt, Willa Cather
From left to right Margaret, Willa,

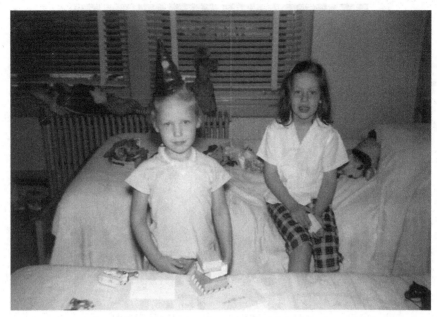

My sister Margaret and me in our shared bedroom

My six little bears Larry, Beary, Harry, Jerry, Gary and Tet Tet Teddy

Our wedding

Rich and Barney, the family dog

Shannon Family at Sun Valley